## About the Author Steven G King

Born in East London 6 years after WW2.
A skinny ginger cockney kid brought up in East London
Was a barrow boy in Petticoat Lane Market.
A trainee cutter of leather & suede.
A messenger for the stock exchange in the City of London.
A computer operator/trainee programmer.
A Roadie for a Band.
Kitchen porter in a hotel, a posh way of saying pot washer.
Husband, Father & Grandfather, living in Yorkshire.
Designer, Shopfitter and Builder. And finally a Dyslexic writer.
Enjoys scuba diving, sailing & cycling-especially in France!
Still building their dream home in south west France.

This is the short version, a lot more has happened
in the last 60 odd years.

Now, let me tell you a story!

_To Darren Vikki Lauren & Emma_
_Have a great 2015_

IBSN-10: 1502962349
IBSN-13: 978-1502962348

Steven G King © 2014

Follow Steven on Twitter
@stevengking_me
www.stevengking.me

In memory of Richard (Dick) Andrews

# Captain's French Adventures

## The Laughter and Lighter Side of French House Hunting, Purchase and Renovation

Illustrations, cartoons and photographs by Steven G King
Cover design by Steven G King

# Absent friends

The devastating news that Dick had cancer and had only just started getting treatment knocked me off my feet.

It only seemed like yesterday, but several months had passed since we were having dinner with our two best friends in our favourite pub restaurant discussing our plans for a possible early retirement. Our children were at home less and looking for their own space. We, on the other hand, all four of us, were rattling around in our big family houses, that we had built ourselves.

I met up with Dick one Saturday morning in his garden. We talked about his future plans of selling his house and building another smaller one on their plot of land next door. We were discussing what trees had to come out and so on, he looked tired as he rested and sat against the bonnet of his car, he complained of severe back ache, I had to keep positive for him in my usual optimistic way but by the time Thursday had arrived that week he was dead!

Some months later, Kath, his wife, put their house on the market and moved to her Spanish holiday apartment to start a new life with her daughters. The memories were too painful living in the house they had put their heart and soul into.

So, for us, we had lost both our friends. It brought home all too clearly the fragility of life. We had often said that life was not a rehearsal but you get deep set in your ways just getting on with the daily grind.

I suppose panic set in for me. Dick's death was never far from my thoughts and I just knew that a lifestyle change had to happen. We couldn't carry on as we were, day in day out chasing our tails with our very busy companies.

# Time for change

It didn't take us long to get our house completely redecorated, into showroom condition and on the market. More panic set in when, after only two weeks, it had sold. We were not ready for leaving the UK for greener pastures yet. We still had a building and shop fitting company and Sue, on the other hand, was very busy in her tea room and gift shop. Besides all that, we were still building the flats above the shop and an extension, this would be our pension when rented out. So deciding to move into a rented house left us mortgage and debt free. It was the best option as it gave us time to explore all avenues of where to go.

I had often wanted to retire to Cyprus. We had had holidays there for many years. It was a very safe place for the boys, but the last holiday Sue had there was awful. I couldn't go because of work and when she got back she completely refused to even consider moving there.

I arrived home from work one evening and spread all over the living room floor were magazines for France and French houses, packed bags and airline tickets. We were flying to Bordeaux on a whistle stop tour of the area house hunting!

# Tearing up the French and German tarmac

We picked up the hire car and headed out on our search for a new home. We had trawled the internet, made a list and checked the prices but we also found a lot of conflicting information. We found diabolically renovated houses and ruins that must have been the dregs of the pile. We spent a lot of time looking for somewhere to eat, places to sleep and most importantly the loos - that weren't convenient and for the most part, definitely not clean.

We must have picked the wrong time to visit some areas. We had torrential rain for nearly a day near Mont-de-Marsan, misty fog in the Dordogne and a flash flood while we visited an Immobilier (estate agent) in Eymet causing a river to flow through the square on market day!

We did have the good fortune to happen upon Monbazillac, well, we drove past the Château and turned around.
We were glad we did. Our first visit to a Château was a very pleasant surprise. What a wonderful place. As we stepped inside we were dwarfed by the gigantic doorway, then overwhelmed by the splendour of the magnificent interior. Impeccable overstated furnishings and décor reaching up to the colossal ceilings. "C'est magnifique" Sue spluttered to the Madam who greeted us. Huge paintings with life-like people, the skin tones and eyes drew you in, captivating your thoughts. Larger than life wardrobes and an enormous stone fireplace, everything was big!

Afterwards we went inside the very tasteful souvenir shop, the intense light streaming through the windows lit up the tiers of bottles containing the golden nectar of the Monbazillac wine, reflecting, casting golden bottle shaped images on various surfaces. We were invited to taste samples offered to us in delicate flute glasses. With one sip, the intensely sweet honey flavour filled my untrained palate, it tasted as good as it looked!

Thankfully the weather had changed. We had a pleasant afternoon in the grounds, wandering through the gardens in the warm sunshine, marvelling at the beautiful preserved architecture.

Our unscheduled indulgence over, we continued our search for a little bit of France, alas to no avail.

We needed to take some time out and recharge. Visiting La Rochelle and staying in a posh hotel certainly did the trick, It just happened to be VE day ( La Fête de la Liberté ) It got us in the holiday mood!

We spoilt ourselves, as the suns rays wrapped around us while we explored the cobbled streets drinking in the atmosphere and listening to the talented buskers, something we appreciate, as both our sons are musicians. Sue indulged in some retail therapy with shoe shopping, while I mused over the expensive boats that lined the marina. The breeze from the sea slapped the halyards against the aluminium masts, playing out a tune, I felt quite at home amongst the yachts.

The French certainly took VE day to their hearts, with a collection of wartime vehicles and their owners dressed in period clothes and uniforms from WW2.

We decided to keep in the holiday mood as we were nearing the end of our stay, so before our flight from Bordeaux we just had to visit Cap Ferret.

I hadn't done any research of the area, it just looked interesting on the map and of course it was the Atlantic Ocean.

The day just couldn't have been better. The cloudless blue sky merged with the blue sea as we strolled down the wooden weathered slatted path between the sand dunes that swept down to the beach from a great height. I was immediately transported back to the mid fifties. After hop picking in Kent our family would spend a day on Camber Sands. The sand dunes were a fantastic playground for us Cockney kids.

It's very strange how something as natural as sand dunes seemed to have popped into my life at various times. Visiting my Nan in Port Talbot South Wales in the fifties, her house was next to the sand dunes, when I first met Sue in 1972 we would spend time on the sand dunes of Woolacombe Bay, North Devon.

We had a great time relaxing, looking at the ocean, while laying on the side of the dunes, the white fine sand of Cap Ferret stretched as far as the eye could see, the beach was almost deserted, the silence broken by the sound of the surf rolling in.

We had to go for a paddle in the ocean. We just couldn't come all this way and not get our feet wet. The water was freezing but exhilarating, the spray moistened our skin and clothes, we walked back to the dunes to dry off in the hot sun.

There was a strange reminder of World War 2, partly submerged pill boxes, concrete stand points occupied by the Germans. The sand had engulfed the remains, the decaying concrete sun bleached structure with brown stains from the exposed steel reinforcing. Visible parts had 21st century colourful graffiti and tags. It seemed a bit odd that they had not been removed from this beautiful place, but then again they were part of the history.

A tiny train ran to and fro from the top of the dunes to the town, we couldn't resist the ride back to civilisation for lunch before departing for the airport.

In just a short time we clocked up 1800 kilometres up and down parts of western France.

Our little taste of France, the first for many years, gave us an insight into what we didn't want in a house and where we didn't want to be. During our flight home we had to rethink our plan. We needed to make it possible to view houses, in some form or other, without all the stress and still have some comfort along the way.

We decided we had to invest in a motorhome. A good plan I thought, but even that presented problems. We went searching in the UK. The only one Sue liked cost in excess of fifty thousand pounds! I couldn't justify that amount of money - we could have bought a small house in Yorkshire for that!

We then looked at several motorhomes with more realistic prices but they were more like sheds on wheels, or so tatty and dirty they needed fumigating. A very informative person on the internet suggested that we go to Germany where the quality and prices were better. We narrowed it down to one motorhome supplier and in no time at all we were on our way to Hanover in northern Germany.

At the sales area in Katlenburg the motorhome we had seen on the internet needed a new shower tray, we didn't want to be using our precious time on repairs, so obviously it wasn't suitable. But whilst looking over the array of vehicles on display we got talking to two men from Norway who were also looking for a motorhome. They told us about another place ninety kilometres further south. We jumped into our hire car and headed south and spent the rest of the day sifting through a hundred or so vehicles. Here they sold ex-rental motorhomes in quantity. Well now we knew again what we didn't want.

After staying overnight, we returned back to Katlenburg to a very surprised dealer. We just had to have another look at what was on offer. The very helpful owner gave us a tray of keys to all the motorhomes and told us to take our time. In and out we went trying to decide. We hadn't come all this way to go back empty handed.

We eventually looked around a big Hymer. It was more than I wanted to pay but, after striking a deal, it was ours. We had a five day wait, checking in and out of motels, waiting for the money to be paid to the dealer, even though our money left our account immediately but never arrived in Germany. British banks will never change.

The process of buying the motorhome was effortless, the Germans being so efficient. Waving goodbye to the dealer we were on our way. I was in the twenty three foot left hand drive motorhome with Sue following me in the hire car. I was very proud of her. It was her first time driving in a foreign country.

Returning the hire car we gingerly entered their office. We had only hired it for a day and nearly a week had passed. We were either naive, or very optimistic, when we first arrived and thought we could do it all in a day. There wasn't a problem as the hire company had been tracking us all the time.

The non-stop journey back to Yorkshire through the night was both hell and great at the same time. At least we had a good motorhome and we had saved fifteen thousand pounds on similar models back in the UK.

## Searching for a little bit of France

Over the next couple of months we got ready for our first epic trip to France. We had a couple of weekend dry runs to North Yorkshire that ended in disaster, a blown tyre that had to be replaced and further punctures that took some sorting out, finally replacing all the tyres on the motorhome just to be safe. We were now getting close to the off.

Embarking into the unknown was exciting. We had packed everything and anything, Sue's sports car was loaded on the trailer ready and waiting, our family was gathered, ready to wave us goodbye. So we pulled out of the drive of the old manor house we were renting, looked back at the smiling faces and headed for the motorway.

The journey south was fairly uneventful, until we joined the M25. We hit a deep rut in the motorway and our motorhome shuddered. As I looked in the wing mirror I saw one of our shiny expensive stainless steel hub caps careering across the motorway. There was no way I could retrieve it.

Arriving in Dover we had some hours to wait for our ferry. We parked in a car park and got settled down. Almost immediately there was someone standing in the car park on their mobile phone and they were having a loud conversation for an hour at 4am! Sue threatened to stick his phone where the sun didn't shine but I pointed out we needed to be in France not spending the day with the police.

It was a beautiful sunny morning as we approached Calais. People were already out beachcombing and fishing. The sandy beaches were a lovely sight from the deck of the ferry. Looking back in our wake we had our first view across the Channel and the cliffs of Dover, what a wonderful sight.

We soon made our way south to Paris. Just a quick stop at an Aire (parking area) to make sure everything was alright with the motorhome and trailer. Every sight we saw was brand new to us although the autoroute was a little boring. We hit the matrix of roads close to Charles de Gaulle airport and took a wrong lane so we ended up having an unscheduled tour of Paris.

It was funny and hair-raising, traffic from all directions on unfamiliar roads, dodging people and mopeds. It was our first visit in twenty six years and it hadn't changed one bit, most cars were full of dents, blimey, they were mad drivers.

We were both tired and hungry, so, stopping in a small street, we got the kettle on and had lunch. The Parisians seemed to find it very amusing. (Les Anglais) We eventually clawed our way through the mayhem of Paris and headed to Orléans.

Sleep deprivation finally hit us as dusk fell. We stopped at an Aire on the autoroute, we were just too exhausted to carry on, but attempting to sleep we found that French cars grow extra doors for slamming just to keep us awake! Is it a conspiracy?

We had a very lazy start to the day, an extended breakfast and a luxurious invigorating hot shower in our motorhome. We were so glad we bought it for our new adventures.

As we crossed one department after another, we climbed the hills and rolled into the deep valleys of the Limousin region towards the Midi Pyrenees like a giant roller coaster reaching a height of 1660 feet above sea level. What views. We saw just a handful of motorhomes heading south, most were going north, holidays over we supposed. We planned to start house hunting in and around Cahors, but by the time we got close it was late evening so we decided to stop at the autoroute services for a much needed rest.

The services were very full, just managing to get a space. As we were getting settled down there was a Tap Tap! on our window. A French truck driver wanted to squeeze his huge truck in behind our motorhome. We had taken up a lot of space at over forty foot long and he wanted us to move up. I obliged, with plenty of gesticulating, handshaking and smiles and he reassured us that he didn't have a noisy refrigeration unit onboard. We eventually had dinner, watched a video, snuggled up under our new duvet and had a very quiet evening and a much needed long, undisturbed sleep!

We only heard a few lorries leave in the early hours out of fifty or so that were parked up!.....The sun came up across the small valley. A church spire opposite was pointing out its direction of travel up into the clear blue sky. There was a slight chill but the brilliant rays were soon upon us. This was the first time we were able to relax since leaving the UK.

Whilst re-fuelling at the pumps, a very big American type RV motorhome with a Smart car attached arrived. The driver, a large English chap with his belly popping out from under his loose crumpled shirt, called over to me while he was waiting to fuel up. He rattled off several names of where he had been and where he was going and made some comments about our trailer. He said, with an air of superiority, that it was easier the way he towed his car. It fell on deaf ears - I hate know-it-alls.

Making our way to Cahors down the steep winding road into the next valley. The approach to the Centre Ville was a problem with its tight corners. Going down a main street with restaurants either side of the road people were sat having late coffee.

They seemed to find our approach quite amusing, nudging and pointing, so we gave them big smiles as we passed slowly by.

Not knowing which way to go in the town we went over one of the bridges that cross the river Lot. The fast flowing, wide river, set in a deep gorge with towering rock faces, was very dramatic and beautiful. What a wonderful place we thought.

Needing the exercise we walked back over the bridge with its very low parapet that separates you from a sheer drop into the water 60 foot below. Not very good if you suffer from vertigo! Searching the old town area for immobiliers (estate agents) we had read about, took us through some lovely old narrow streets. This was our first taste of a French town since arriving.

Peering through the windows of the immobiliers, like little children looking in a sweet shop, with our noses pressed against the glass, we caught an agent's eye. She beckoned us in. We obviously looked very green around the ears. The English agent seemed a little patronising when we got talking about prices. I may have looked fresh and green and unable to speak French but being a cockney I was very street wise and saw through how they operate.

Prices were mostly hiked up for the unsuspecting Brit. Also, houses sometimes had been bought by an associate of the immobilier at a knock down price then sold on.

A case of insider trading. We weren't parting with our hard earned cash on this basis.

It was of no surprise that houses advertised on the internet didn't represent what was actually for sale in France and the web sites seemed out of date by several months. We were not disappointed as we were realists. We didn't want to pay these sort of prices, we weren't desperate, something would turn up.

It was a beautiful sunny day and we didn't have to rush anywhere. We had no appointments to keep, time was ours. Looking around the old town with its narrow medieval backstreets was how we imagined the architecture would be. We bought some provisions, stumbling with our terrible French. We called in at the tourist office situated on the edge of town, the lady said we could help ourselves to the leaflets and maps on display, she wished us bon voyage as we left carrying a good handful.

Returning to our motorhome on the other side of the bridge we were greeted by a Frenchman and his wife. They also had a Hymer motorhome. It was our first encounter with a French family on holiday. They were very friendly and told us enthusiastically where to visit. "Panorama magnifique" ! "We must visit Rocamadour – très bon".
Despite his pigeon English and our terrible French the language barrier didn't matter, the smiles and handshakes said it all.

We had a late lunch and went back to the town to see the immobiliers that were closed previously. It was still the same story.

We decided to make our way to Moisac, further south, where there was a farmhouse for sale. It looked interesting and was at a price we were willing to pay. It was getting late and darkness growing. The sun just drops out of the sky in this part of the world.

Driving down a narrow winding road where huge articulated trucks trundled along at great speed in the pitch black darkness was bit unsettling. Suddenly we happened upon an Aire on the edge of a small town called Montcuq. We missed the entrance but pulled into a small petrol station. We did a U turn through it and parked up for the night. I got Sue settled in and decided to walk down to get some parking tokens from the petrol station and there I met the young owner Deni and his family. He was an encyclopedia of information, he spoke very good English and he had worked in many places in the south west. He said before we leave he would give us some advice on good areas to search when I explained why we were in France.

The next morning we walked to the centre ville of Montcuq for some bread and discovered to our surprise a very quaint and medieval town with it's little back streets, steep climbs, overhanging buildings and quite a few immobiliers. We decided to stay and look for property in this area.

After noting down several houses we returned to the motorhome and took Sue's car off the trailer. It was 25 deg and a beautiful blue sky. So Sue got her top off!

Hymer at Jardin des Causses Nr Cahors

# Ever increasing circles

We went in search of our new home in Sue's open top sports car. We looked at some in our price range but found them unsuitable. One house, a ruin for complete restoration, was next to a very messy farm with cow pats everywhere and flies!

We soon realised that this area is very pricey. It seems there are a lot of English around and this hypes up the prices in some cases to nearly double!

We were warned that the coming weekend was the annual 200km Montcuq endurance horse race and hence the Aire where we were parked was the designated horse box park. An expected 200 or so of them were due to roll in!

Visiting different houses with the agents gave us the same impression that the properties we were shown were difficult to sell. We saw the same houses advertised with several agents and in just a short time it was obvious how the industry worked.

After fruitlessly tearing around the countryside we decided to return to our motorhome and turn in for the night.

The next morning, sure enough, the Aire started to fill up. To escape the commotion we went out to look at another house. The English agent didn't seem to understand the English words for not remote and not next to a livestock farm. Again it was totally unsuitable.

On returning to our motorhome it was surrounded by horse boxes and 4x4s. We decided we had to move but the municipal campsite opposite was closed for the season. We got ready to leave and loaded up the car. Within moments of our moving another 4x4 with a horse box attached raced into our spot.

We were glad to be leaving the area. Oh! The French interpretation of the town Montcuq sounds like "MY ARSE" which left us laughing as we made our way to Montpezat du Quercy to a new campsite.

Arriving at the campsite the owner tells us that he will be closing in a few days for the winter. The campsite is deserted, it's very strange.

We are getting used to where everything is placed in our motorhome, but we do get the odd surprise. We must remember that after arriving somewhere new there will be the odd tin of beans or jar of honey ready to launch itself at us from the overhead lockers! Sometimes for a split second we breathe a sigh of relief as it lands on the soft seating below, but this is short lived, as it bounces and does a backwards somersault, like some Olympic high diver. Up in the air it goes and comes crashing down on an unsuspecting foot - ouch!

As you can imagine it is very quiet.

We visit an immobilier just across from the campsite. The agent, Bridget, originally from Denmark, seems to be on our wavelength. She said prices are falling as her clients are saying drop the price! This is contrary to what other agents have tried to make us believe, giving us some confidence in her.

She sends us to a house that she thinks will be exactly what we want. It's not far from the town. When we arrived it appeared to be just perfect. Away from the main road with it's own private approach, great views and in pretty good condition. It seemed too good to be true! We discovered a young French couple restoring it. They had bought it some months earlier. The owner had sold it to them direct and failed to tell Bridget. That's one way to save paying their fees!

Just a little disheartened, we soon picked ourselves up and got on with the search, spending the next few days driving around the countryside with the top down in temperatures around the 25 deg. A phone call back to our two sons in the UK said it has been raining heavily for a couple of days - one more tick in the plus box for moving to France.

The beautiful rolling countryside of this area with it's magnificent views, small medieval towns, free parking, laid back attitude, friendly service in shops, the way the young and old greet each other, and us, with friendly respect makes the UK seem a little hostile at times. Compare the

UK with it's big brother CCTV, speed cameras around every corner, traffic wardens lurking and waiting to pounce at the mere hint of leaving your car for a couple of minutes where it shouldn't be or slapping a £30 fine for overstaying at a car park for those extra few seconds. France will have it's faults no doubt but at least the sun is shining.

At the deserted campsite the autumn leaves are falling, the church bell chimes on the hour through the night, the wind gets up and the surrounding trees sway and rustle. A family of magpies have the odd chatter to each other breaking the silence. A far cry from the hustle and bustle of what this place must be like in full summer with it's communal barbeque, children's swings and play area in the centre of the sloping terrain campsite. It's very eerie.

We decide to have a meal out on the recommendation of our friendly campsite owner Monsieur Bro. That was a big mistake as they could only offer us a cold meat salad. In the bar there were just some young people talking at the next table. We were a little apprehensive but thought - they can't mess up a salad can they? Oh, yes they can. It was disgusting and on top of that, it wasn't cheap!

Montpezat was another medieval town with restored colombage buildings. Very tidy, clean and friendly. The architecture made up for our disappointing escapades. As we explored the tiny streets that opened out to a lovely square surrounded by tall buildings with newly cleaned impressive stonework, a little butcher's shop caught our eye with an impressive display of meat in the window. It must have been popular as there was a queue waiting to be served inside. I looked at Sue and asked if we should get something for dinner. We went inside and as we joined the queue everyone turned to us and said "Bonjour". We both replied with a cheerful "bonjour" and waited our turn.

I looked over my shoulder and saw a very small, very old, lady slightly hunched over with a black scarf and a big black shopping bag over her arm. She was wrestling with the door latch trying to hold her bag and her walking stick all at the same time. I turned, opened the door and beckoned her in. Before anyone else could speak I blurted out in my cockney accented French " Bonjour mademoiselle". A couple of seconds of silence was followed by roars of laugher from the whole shop, including the old lady. Sue nudged me in the ribs. I turned to her and said "What" ? I think it was one of my Delboy moments!

We called back to see Bridget, she was surprised at the news that the house had been sold. She told us of another house requiring renovation that was in a beautiful location. We got our hopes up as we drove across country to Caylus. A beautiful, partly restored medieval town situated on a horseshoe hillside, first settled in 12AD with outstanding views on the approach.

The property was further north in a forest area. She told us the house could be wonderful when restored. When we got to the area it was very remote. We drove along an unmade and rutted dirt single track that never seemed to end. With the forest towering above us on both sides we eventually found the house.

You have to imagine the film set of the Temple of Doom from Indiana Jones. The very large ruin had four walls and no roof but it did have huge trees growing in the entire house. Everything was covered in vines and vegetation. The wood had engulfed the whole area. The only thing that would clear this lot was dynamite!

Another wasted journey. The agents just aren't listening to us and it seems to be the norm. It still hits a nerve though.

Back at the campsite we have some heavy rain, but the sun does come out and it isn't cold. During the day we are searching for empty houses and making enquires as to whether they are for sale.

This region is not cheap but it does have some of the best weather throughout the year. We are making new contacts every day and getting used to finding our way around.

The rolling countryside is very tidy, with its small towns perched on the hills and villages nestling in the valleys. There is a new view around every hillside. A perfect backdrop for any landscape artist.

Monsieur Bro calls by to say his neighbour's mother and father are selling their farmhouse not far from town. We agree to follow him to have a look.

I have been driving for over 37 years and seen hundreds of the caution road sign triangles with the silhouette of a prancing deer, even the Moose type in New England. But never have I seen one animal. As we drove out of the town and down the hill a large wild deer paused at the roadside, looked up at us, hopped across the road and bounced over the field eventually disappearing into a wood. We looked on in amazement, while Monsieur Bro carried on driving as if nothing had happened.

We parked outside the very old farmhouse and were greeted by an even older owner.

We entered through the kitchen which resembled a squalid squat in East London. Hanging from the low ceiling were rows of fly papers with hundreds of dead flies stuck to them. On the kitchen table it looked like the old lady was preparing to make something with apples. They were piled high in a big bowl and were a dark shade of rotting brown, tiny flies surrounded the disgusting heap. The doorways had heavy dirty cloths hanging from them, perhaps to keep the cold out, or the flies in. Who knows!

We were courteous and had a look around. The barn was huge with an impressive timber roof structure. I suppose we could have demolished the house and lived in the barn. It came to the question of price. The old lady looked at us and looked at Sue's gleaming silver sports car, that must have had a flashing neon £ sign on the roof. The little old lady rubbed her hands together, grabbed her calculator and keyed in the price. We looked at each other. We knew what we were both thinking - dream on old girl - and that was that. We left.

## A change for the better but not the weather

The weather had changed overnight. It started getting very cold and wet. The campsite closure was imminent so we loaded up the car onto the trailer, said our goodbyes to Monsieur Bro and made our way to Cayriech in the darkness to the only campsite that was open during winter.

We arrived in Cayriech after navigating the steep, winding, narrow but thankfully deserted roads across country from Montpezat. We took a right turn in the village but we were not sure where the campsite was. Stopping at a junction we rang the owner. After getting directions (in French) we had to turn round on the narrow lane. It was very dark and raining and even with our infra-red reversing camera it was very difficult to see.

As usual whenever we have to turn round, cars come from everywhere. It was like Piccadilly Circus. We had to sit there on the corner whilst they all squeezed passed us. Just then a van pulled up and a little Frenchman beckoned us to follow him. It was the campsite owner who had come out to look for us. What a nice chap.

We pulled into the campsite. It was a bit of a squeeze as the entrance wasn't designed for vehicles as long as ours. We had to do a wide turn into the designated motorhome area. All the spaces were full so we had to manoeuvre around and park in the centre. We got hooked up with power and settled in for the night. The rain was still lashing it down.

In the morning the sun was back. Thank goodness!

A space occupied by a couple staying overnight, who were on their way back to Manchester, was becoming vacant. So after a brief hello goodbye we moved into it. I noticed a trail of thick mud along the long driveway. It led to our trailer. I followed it back along the drive and found that in the darkness we had driven over the campsite owners beautifully manicured garden. We had left a deep rut. He was making ready with his gardening tools to fix the damage. I offered to help and he said "D'accord" (It's ok). I felt a plonker but after all he was guiding us with his torch!

The sun was shining with temperatures in the twenties. It is a holiday, a day of remembrance so everything is closed. We decided to go for a power walk. We needed some exercise as we are not used to spending so much time sitting and driving. After 6.5 miles we arrived back in a sweat.

We said hello to our travelling neighbours, introducing themselves, Peter and Eileen were from Lancaster. They are on their way to Spain to spend winter in the sun and then returning to the UK next May. They are a very nice easy-to-get-along with couple slightly older than ourselves. During our stay we were to get through quite a few bottles! Many a good chinwag! And plenty of laughter!

Cayriech is a small, pretty but growing village. The church which is the focal point dates back to the last Gothic period. It was demolished during the War of Religions but was restored during the 17th century.

A restoration project of the dilapidated and neglected buildings in the early nineties was the passion of Jeanine Mulpas (Mayoress). She has instigated a regime of respect for the land which includes promoting organic cultivation and recycling. Well, quite a green type of person. The village has won several national awards, the latest was the Concours Européen de l'Entente Florale 2004

From our campsite the town of Puylaroque can be seen about four kilometres away. It's high up on a hill with its white stone walls and towering church spire. From the grounds there is a vantage point giving breathtaking panoramic views of the surrounding area and beyond to the Pyrénées. The town has a few shops and restaurants. By night the entire church and perimeter area is illuminated by powerful sodium flood up lighters and the white stone radiates a golden glow which can be seen for miles around beckoning the weary traveller.

The nearest busy market town of Caussade is to the south and has all the usual commerce!

We decide to stay on at the quiet and safe campsite of Cayriech. With our Hymer motorhome as a base and use Sue's car to fan out over the surrounding area, so we were racing about looking at houses, ruins, land - well anything really.

The winter is setting in now so it's cold at night and sometimes there's early morning mist but the sun does eventually come out. We made the long journey to Moisac to view a farmhouse that was advertised on the internet. It looked impressive with towers at each end but when we arrived we couldn't have felt more deflated. The crumbling ruin was sat in a sea of rubbish. Strewn around was old machinery and some very botched repairs to the crumbling stonework which was a nice shade of grey concrete.

I think the photographs were taken when the structure was first built, or the photographer was very creative. There was no building just the two towers connected by a bit of dodgy stonework.

Another farm house we visited in the area was made of mud bricks that were eroding away. The agent tried her best to convince us it would be lovely when it was finished. Urgggggg!

We have been visiting more so called estate agents and decided that these people are extremely disorganised, they just seem to muddle through. Sue is getting upset by the incompetence. We agree to look at two more houses and then either we will move to another area or go home.

At the agents office the young English girl gave us a scrap of paper with an address and a map. We made our way carefully following the map. We drove up and down a long road passing the same junction several times. I was looking for an "ICI" sign as marked on the map with an X. Up and down we went. I finally worked out, after I stopped a passing motorist, that the road we wanted was very close. The motorist seemed very confused with my questions about an "ICI" sign. I couldn't understand why but you can work this out for yourself!

We found the house. It almost had a river running through it. It was a mess and had pigeons living in it. We made our way to the second house. It was very remote. Now, if I were into extreme sports it would have been ideal. At least, once the pile of stone had been turned into a house then I would have been able to run out of the front door, launch myself off a sheer cliff and soar away into the sky.

We went back to Cayriech and sanity.

## It never seems to end

Thinking the worst was over and things could only get better. It seemed we were in luck. A young lady returned our telephone call and she invited us to her house on Sunday. She said she had two properties that were just what we were looking for. We got excited, not very excited, but excited just the same.

It was a beautiful sunny Sunday morning. We told Peter and Eileen about our good fortune and we roared out of the campsite, waving as we went, full of anticipation. We arrived at the ramshackle house and surroundings. Our expectations waned slightly. She was a very nice helpful young lady and she asked us to stay and have lunch. We were a little taken aback but we agreed.

We learnt that she made goats cheese in the mornings and in the afternoons she was an estate agent. She was very busy running around preparing everything. Her partner meanwhile was close to being horizontal and puffing away on his hand rolled cigarette - or was it something stronger? He reminded us of a spaced out Dylan, the rabbit off the Magic Roundabout. She was certainly the driving force of the family.

Lunch over we went to see her associate. He was a French builder living nearby. We couldn't see the connection but we followed in our car anyway. Once there, we were shown around his house which he was in the process of rebuilding. Still puzzled we went with the flow. We were sat down and given coffee and chit chat. We looked at each other wondering when we were going to look at houses. We eventually said we had a further appointment later in the day and we better get moving and look at the houses she told us about.

We were told to follow them as they both jumped into their white Berlingo van. At this point we were not sure if the sight of Sue's sports car stirred something in the loins of the Frenchman, or that he was lacking something in size, but he started his engine and raced out of his dusty drive on two wheels, leaving us behind in a cloud of dust. It wasn't difficult keeping up with him but Sue screamed at me as she bounced and almost flew out of her seat on the bumpy roads, "slow down! slow down and let him have his fun."

He was driving like a lunatic on the single track high hedged roads, clipping the hedges at times with the back of his van. We kept a safe but visible distance. If he meets something big and solid at least we will be able to stop I told Sue, her fingernails imbedded in the seat and holding on for dear life. We seemed to be following him in ever decreasing circles until he turned sharp right. I looked at Sue "This road looks familiar," I said as we turned into a grassy drive. We were at the house with the river and pigeons!

We got out of our car, I clenched Sue's hand and said "Keep schtum"! We didn't waste any time and said it was unsuitable. They tried to convince us that it was a great house with potential. No we didn't like it. "Ok," they said, "we will go to the other house."

Off they went at break neck speed on another white knuckle ride around the French countryside with us following. Around and around we went, up and down the country lanes. We were pleased it was a Sunday, at least the roads were quiet. The little van flew up a narrow road and disappeared over a hill leaving a flurry of leaves in the air and scattering loose stones on the road. I shouted "Oh no". We were at the house that was a pile of stone on a cliff edge we had seen days earlier.

The mad Frenchman attempted to drive up to the cliff on the steep unmade limestone track. He got stuck halfway up, his front wheel drive tyres were digging up the track and spitting stones out like bullets. We had to laugh or we would have cried. We made our excuses and left them at the launching pad.

## Sous le nez

Peter and Eileen made us feel a whole lot better when we arrived back at the campsite and told them about the frustrating day over a cup of tea. Peter cheered us up with a big grin "We had a lovely cycle ride in the sunshine, a nice coffee at Septfonds village, you should have come" he said. He ducked, expecting Sue to tip her tea over his head.

Having a motorhome is not just a means of getting from A to B, somewhere to sleep etc, but also making friends along the way, laughing, reminiscing, putting the world to rights. Age is not a barrier. We have also had the unsociable types that pass through with the, my motorhome is bigger, newer, than yours and I am better than you. It's their sad loss. We have had the same experience when sailing. They miss all the fun and friendship.

We were a little down in the dumps with all the false hopes. Our planned departure date had passed and we had decided to stay a little longer in the hope it would give us more time to search.

Peter & Eileen had decided to stay as well to keep us company. But sadly time is running out. Although Sue has left her busy shop in capable hands it does need her personal touch running up to Christmas. She is getting a little despondent. After 33 years of marriage we know how each other ticks. I am pretty optimistic and tell her something will turn up, thankfully she doesn't notice my crossed fingers behind my back.

An early morning start. I pulled back the thermal screens and opened the curtains to a beautiful sunny morning. Peter & Eileen were getting ready for a shopping trip to Caussade, 10 minutes away. They persuaded us to join them in their motorhome. I imitated a Lancashire accent and said, "I'll be Max and you can be Paddy" (Peter Kay). We all had a laugh. We just had to lift our spirits somehow.

Meandering through the market stalls, the unfamiliar sights and smells were fascinating. Buying our produce with our embarrassingly poor French, the stallholders didn't seem to mind they just smiled and were delighted to help us.

Looking around the town's backstreets took me back to the 50's & 60's of East London markets where I worked as a barrow boy for my Granddad in Petticoat Lane. The chattering between the stall holders and customers was a delight to listen to, their facial expressions and hand gestures seemed very passionate as they talked about the produce, at least, it seemed that way. There was an abundance of fresh fruit and vegetables some complete with soil. One delicatessen stall had a huge selection of pickles, chillies & olives next to baskets full of colourful dried peppers. You could serve yourself with a tub and spoon, or as some ladies did, they just pulled out handfuls.

Further along the tiny backstreet there was a long low stall full of spices from around the world, they were displayed in open wicker baskets and various open tiny sacks. Everything on display, said, this is all natural, the mixture of colours, were like an abstract painting. Our gaze was drawn by the variety of smells from the chilli & turmeric to the vanilla pods that just made you lick your lips.

Cheese aficionados would be in their element, the huge refrigerated stall was crammed packed. The stall holder offered you samples to try, passing them to us on the end of his very sharp knife, we just had to buy some!

Making our way to the main square and parking area that is given over to huge articulated lorries, they were like a tardis, the sides opened upwards to make a roof and the backs slid out, almost doubling in size, hey presto! It's a travelling shoe shop. Another sold pots and pans, the ingenious traders had fitted arms that pulled out complete with whatever is being sold attached. I had never seen anything like it.

We finished our shopping with bags laden in hand, we made our way in search of a much needed coffee and a sit down. We were planning to stop at one of the cafés that line the town's streets. We were just about to sit down when Sue exclaimed that the shiny stainless steel seats were freezing cold. Peter then guided us to a small hotel that he'd visited the year before set in the backstreets.

They had a wonderful blazing fire and it was very cosy drinking our coffee. Suddenly Sue noticed an immobilier across the road. We thought we had exhausted all the agents in Caussade but we hadn't seen this one tucked away.

I believe in fate and coincidences and today was no exception. Peering through the window at the numerous properties for sale a couple caught our eye. We decided to go in and enquire. The very nice proprietor spoke little English but he gave us directions to one of the properties. We were surprised that it was on the edge of Cayriech. "Cayriech?" we said. "Oui" he replied. We were knocked sideways.

We eagerly returned to Cayriech, parked up on the campsite, had lunch and then the four of us went in search of the mill ruin and grange that was situated at the back of the church. As we approached we could see the grange and a sign saying private entry. We climbed over the low fence and made our way to the mill. Only the front and rear walls to the 1st floor and the two gable ends were left standing. The rest was gone. Rotting timbers, vegetation, a couple of large cart wheels and heavy steel axles were littered inside together with the two, still intact, huge mill stones. The main lower structure was in very good shape. The stone arch through which the water flowed was in perfect condition. We noticed a faint date over one of the solid stone door lintels of the grange - 1780. The mill we believe is older.

We were drawn to the sound of running water. It was out of sight of the mill. As we reached the river bank the water was cascading over the falls. It was very tranquil, picturesque, well everything beautiful all rolled into one! Water to the mill was via a tributary from the main river, passing under a single arch below the house and rejoining the river further downstream.

We made our way back to the campsite and that evening we had a get-together with a bottle or two and talked over the possibilities.

The next morning the Immobilier called to pick us up as arranged. He took us to see another property, a large grange on a smallish plot. The property was built from the reclaimed stone of an ancient church, complete with gargoyles. It was on the side of a hill and a little remote and very windy. We said it wasn't suitable but the price was good.

Arriving back at Cayriech, the immobilier showed us around the mill explaining what came with it. He pointed to the grange, this plot and then that plot, the river and the canal, we thought we were dreaming. It took our breath away. I could see the potential straight away. Yes it was a complete re-build but the location was superb. We had neighbours but not too close, we could walk to the village to hopefully enjoy village life.

We said our goodbyes to Monsieur Larroque and started to daydream for a short time while explaining to Sue what we could achieve with some hard work!

The weather in Cayriech is changeable but mostly dry. There's an abundance of wildlife; several resident birds of prey, a pair of green woodpeckers and one morning a pair of kites made a low pass heading west into the mist. We have the usual cheeky robin outside the motorhome and the odd cat foraging.

In just a short time we seem to be getting into the French way of life, although we haven't escaped the car with the large rear can speakers blasting out boom-boom-boom as he passes daily. Probably making his way to the hearing aid shop in the next town. We must be getting old!

The Mill as it stands is too small for us. In France it is necessary to see the mayor to discuss anything that concerns the village, buildings, well just about anything. So I rang the mayor of Cayriech at her home to make an appointment. She sounded very nice. She didn't speak English and I didn't speak French but we had a good laugh. She must have understood some of my gibberish because she sent a message, via the campsite owner, with our appointment time!

We went forearmed with perspective sketches of the proposed rebuilding works. It's what I do for a living in the UK so luckily for us it was a bonus. Our audience with the Mayoress included the immobilier, Peter and Eileen and the campsite owner, who happened to be the local councillor, so we had our own little army fighting our corner.

We were ushered into a very grand long room. It was immaculate. Beautiful stone walls, a highly polished huge central long table, there were so many chairs I couldn't count them, pictures on the wall of the current President of France, past Mayors and French flags. One very important item proudly on display was the concours award for best village.

My drawing was on quite a large scale and it brought the mill and grange together with a colombage archway. As normal with planners and officials a deep breath was drawn and shaking of heads but, after negotiations, a scaled down version was agreed upon. That was our pre-requisite prior to making an offer on the mill. We surprised ourselves coping with the language barrier, as we left, Madam Mulpas took great pride in presenting Sue with a beautiful glossy book of the Village, it showed before and after pictures of the village renovation, what a lovely gesture.

We visited the immobilier the next day and made a cast iron offer the owner could not refuse. The property had only just come onto the market within the last two weeks and it was sure to have been snapped up because of its location and keen price. He wanted to give us a two week cooling off period but we said it was not necessary - we wanted it.

L'ancien Moulin (ruin) Cayriech               Watercolour by Kim Prior

# Sad goodbyes

We bid a fond farewell to Peter & Eileen, our motorhome neighbours and new found friends for the last fortnight. They had to make their way to Spain before the snow set in over the mountains. Later that evening we decided to go out for a meal to a new posh restaurant and celebrate. It was a few minutes away in Puylaroque. Another expensive disaster. I think I should open a place of my own. Although we did not complain, the meals were far too arty farty and fussy, not very well made, the meat was tough and my snails were bland. The young lady serving us was very nice, friendly and helpful, I only wish Gordon Ramsey could give them some advice. The place was empty apart from one Danish couple. My wife serves better meals at her tea room back in Yorkshire! We returned to Cayriech. The sky was clear and a very bright full moon lit our way back. We were in for a cold night!

We awoke to a bitterly cold morning. A pack of water left outside is now six 2 litre ice lollies. A clear blue sky, a heavy frost sparkling in the rising sunlight and a full moon still clearly visible high in the west. The campsite is now almost deserted. Just one other lonesome motorhome traveller in remission with cancer, an extremely sad tale. It reminded us of our best and only friend lost to cancer. His wife now living in Spain. This is the whole point of why we are here - a complete lifestyle change.

We are getting ready to leave for Yorkshire. Taking down the satellite dish, stowing everything away, emptying tanks, filling with gallons of water for our long journey back home 1400 kilometres away, we hope it doesn't take to long to get the deal done.

Monsieur Larroque our immobilier as it turned out was very well connected, he arranged very quickly a survey for termites, lead, and asbestos all without a hitch, a pre-purchase obligation by the buyer. Monsieur Larroque explained in his pigeon English that arranging a meeting with a Notaire (solicitor) would be difficult with such short notice. We explained we had to return to the UK, he said " I elp you" his attempt at English was endearing.

The Notaires are servants of the government and act for both parties impartially. As Monsieur Larroque put it, they are very "important man" and very busy. We had faith that our luck had certainly changed. We left it in Monsieur Larroque's capable hands.

The next day Monsieur Larroque telephoned. He was able to get a late evening meeting with his good friend and very important man, the Notaire, at the end of the week. We telephoned our bank to forewarn them of the house purchase.

It was lovely just to be able to relax after all the dashing about house hunting. We could now telephone the family back home and give them the good news. The questions flooded back over the mobile phone. Where is it? What sort of house? Can you move into it? And so on.

We explained that it needed re-building but was a fantastic location with its own river. Rory our youngest piped up "Are there fish in the river? Can we fish it? Have you seen any big ones" In another breath, "when are you coming home" To think they are both in their late twenties, still at home, still our boys. Lovely!

Over the next few days it was difficult not to keep going down to our ancient Moulin. We just kept standing looking, getting excited at the thought of building our new home here. It was, I suppose, quite romantic, a new start in a new country, new challenge. I thought back to the old TV programme the Good Life, living off the land as much as possible. We, as a family, lived a very healthy lifestyle in the UK. Both boys could cook from scratch, Sue had seen to that, so it was nothing new to us.

We had both reached a junction, where we had accomplished most of what we set out to do in life. Or I should say, life steered us through to this point. It's just that you reach a certain age and think time is rushing by.

Monsieur Larroque telephoned to confirm our late evening meeting with the Notaire. It was the only time available and he told us to meet him at his office in Caussade. We then followed Monsieur Larroque in our car to Albias, ten minutes away. The office was quite ordinary and modern. We were surprised the staff we still there and very busy so late. Clients were sat waiting to see the Notaire. We were in for a long wait.

Finally, it was our turn. Entering an office that had piles of paperwork on top of every available space. The Notaire looked every bit a very busy important man. He was also a lovely ordinary man, short and stocky with a very kind rounded face. His glasses perched on the end of his nose as he peered over them to welcome us with a cheerful "Bonsoir".

He spoke only a little English. It was a very straightforward transaction, although I did point out that everything was subject to us getting the correct paperwork for us to be able to re-build. There wasn't a problem. He had a copy of a CU certificate for us. The previous owner, another very important man, had obtained one. The Certificat D'Urbanisme enabled the land and buildings to be deemed for habitation and was last inhabited during the second world war. The only other document required was the Permis de construire - the building permit once our plans were passed. I was so pleased that I had read up on as much information on French house purchase and building prior to leaving the UK.

We signed for the mill and paid our 5% deposit, It was ours, we looked at each other beaming and I said "That's it, it's all go now".

We drove back to the now deserted campsite which was a very strange sight. We turned in for the night full of excitement, and a little apprehension. It's only natural, its a big move into the unknown. We had a lot to learn, and not just French.

The next day there was one final job before leaving Cayriech. We just had to get plenty of photos and a video of our new purchase. This was a Specific instruction given to us by everyone back in Yorkshire. We measured up the mill and grange so that I could prepare the drawings back home. We loaded Sue's car on the trailer, said our goodbyes to the campsite owner and then made our way north, leaving behind clear blue skies and a glorious winter setting sun.

The roads were very quiet. The further north we got the colder it was getting. We decided to give the Paris roads a miss and went via Rouen. A very heavy, severe frost had caused all the trees to ice up. The landscape looked like a film from the ice age. It was quite a relief to get back to Yorkshire where it was certainly warmer. Our welcome home was equally warm as the whole family had gathered to savour our tales - and what tales we had to tell them!

# Excitingly good news

The telephone rang one afternoon at Sue's tea room. The French voice said "Bonjour Mrs King". It wasn't expected. We had read and were told about the slow progress of the French Bureaucracy, so it was a surprise when Monsieur Larroque said that the Notaire had rung to say our paperwork for the purchase of our Moulin was ready for completion. This news was fantastic, it gave us a good excuse to have another trip to France.

The mammoth task of loading the motorhome with everything and anything for a long stay was daunting. We had been busy buying gardening stuff, lots of it, petrol strimmers, loppers and cutters, my building gear, including surveying equipment, was slowly being squeezed into every available space.

By mid July it was time to leave. The family had gathered once again to see us off from our rented house. The motorhome and car was packed to bursting so with waves, smiling faces and our youngest son shouting, "Don't forget to come back," we set off from Barnsley where for a change we had a bright sunny evening.

Leaving ourselves plenty of time for a leisurely drive down to Dover seemed a good idea but, as usual, the UK roads had so many repairs going on we only just made the ferry to Dunkirk, arriving in the early hours. During the journey down we had several heated conversations, albeit light hearted, about things we had forgotten to pack. One main item was a new

French map to get us around the Paris roads. We didn't want a repeat performance of last year - but it wasn't me!

Now on French soil and making our way to Paris, where we hoped we wouldn't make the same mistake as last time, the excitement and lack of sleep caught up with us. We just had to stop at an Aire and rest. The early morning sun was rising fast, the light trying to kid our minds that we had slept, our bodies telling us differently, we drew the screens fitted the roof light blinds, leapt into bed and drifted off to sleep.

Some hours later, we were awoken by very noisy traffic and heat. We opened the window screens and the sun burst in. Squinting out into the intense light and peering across the autoroute heading north the traffic had ground to a halt.

People were out of their cars and looking up the carriageway in a hope that they could see an end to the delay. Thankfully we were going the other way.

After a very late breakfast, that was more like lunch, we headed off on our way southwards. The temperature was rising with every kilometre the deeper we got into France. By the time we hit the Paris ring road Sue was sitting in her knickers and tee shirt, her feet resting in a bowl of cold water whilst cooling herself down with a wet flannel. It was something to do with the weather or the menopause. Don't go there!

The sun was relentless, as each truck passed we were blasted with furnace-like heat through the windows from their overheating engines. It was quite unbearable.

Making good progress things were going well. Then! Whiz, crack, whine. Something was wrong. The noise seemed to be coming from under the motorhome. As luck would have it, there was a services in the distance Pulling in I had to investigate what was causing the noise. I found it was a central bearing on our prop shaft. The grease casing had blown apart probably caused by the extreme heat. Thankfully, the bearing itself was ok.

I was laying under our motorhome, in cream trousers and white tee shirt, shouting, "can you hear me now?" as I tried to communicate with the Mercedes dealer in Sheffield. It's always the same when you need a mobile phone to work at a crucial moment. A couple of French truck drivers were watching me ducking in and out from under the motorhome. By now I was covered in grease and they seemed to find it very amusing.

Finally, I was able to sort the problem out and get cleaned up to carry on our way.

The heat does funny things to your mind. The sat nav was telling me to turn off onto the next autoroute. I started to argue with it saying "shut up, you've got it wrong." It kept repeating the same message, then, as I went the way I wanted to, it started to say, "Recalculating, recalculating." "Shut up, shut up," I said. I was ready for throwing it out of the window.

After a short detour! We got on our way, the sat nav won! Sue kept quiet.

The unbearable 100 degrees heat was relentless. There was no point in stopping to rest, we just had to get further south and head for the hills. Reaching the Limousin region and climbing to over a thousand feet the air was a little cooler. The sun started to set as we pulled off the road into an Aire for the night. Parking up, suddenly the sky went black and an almighty storm flew through. Hail and rain going sideways rocked our motorhome. Ten minutes and it was gone, leaving fresher air which meant we could get a good night's sleep.

Our hopes for some rest were short lived when two huge trucks pulled in next to us with refrigerated cargo, the noise from their engines was going to keep us awake all night. After supper, the car park further away had emptied. We moved as quickly as possible. Even though we were taking up six car park bays we didn't care, we needed to sleep in peace.

Long into a deep sleep, I had a very strange dream of children running, laughing and playing. Then the motor home rocked several times. I wasn't dreaming. I looked at the clock it was 1am. Looking outside, "What the bloody hell," I cried. Small children were jumping up and down on our trailer. The parents looking on found it very amusing. Seeing me they called them back in an eastern European accent. I was still dazed from lack of sleep, slumping back in bed I went into a comatose state.

Approach to Cayriech. The lovingly tendered park on the right is the handy-work of the Village gardeners and the enthusiastic village residents.

Our grange adjacent to the Moulin. It will be our summer kitchen and workshop..........Well after some hard work.

# A fresh start

A beautiful summer morning, the air was fresh with that earthy smell after rain, looking out over the breathtaking views from the Aire that was perched on a hill top was a welcome sight, early travellers were sitting at the communal tables tucking into food produced from their cool boxes, others getting exercise with their dogs, calling out a cheerful "Bonjour" to us as they passed, with inquisitive looks at our home on wheels, a very pleasant start to the day.

Cayriech, now just several hours away, the unscheduled plan of getting this far south enabled us to have a relaxing drive taking in the outstanding beautiful scenery, after a short stop for lunch, we were soon entering the Midi Pyrenees, the temperature still in the 90's, our long journey through stunning countryside and views so far and wide as the eye could see, no camera could capture the vastness of it in one take, the light is so different in these parts, brighter, crisper.

Driving on the new toll road that cuts through the landscape it reduces our journey time but also means we missed interesting towns and villages along the way, we would have to allow an extra week to our journey as we just wouldn't be able to resist the urge to go exploring around every corner.

Leaving the autoroute and paying our dues at the péage we headed for the town centre of Caussade to call at the Intermarche, we needed to replace the six two litre bottles of water that we had perspired during our journey, the supermarket set in tree lined grounds gave us some welcome shade, with the odd banana tree here and there, giving a very Mediterranean feel, it brought back memories of many happy holidays spent in Cyprus, now a little spoilt by us Brits almost taking over entire villages, in one village where we stayed, nearly seventy five percent are English with not much integration with the Cypriots, our Greek friends do resent it.

## Cayriech stirring our emotions

The last few kilometres filled us with mixed emotions, not knowing what to expect as we neared the village, it was just as we remembered it, quiet, picturesque and extremely clean, crossing over the little stone humpback bridge revealed that the village was in bloom and summer was here, every planter and border was full of pansies surrounded by daisy's of every description broken up with clumps of rosemary, there were delicate trumpet shaped deep red flowers cascading over the tubs, I am not a gardener but I can appreciate the work that has gone into preparing the village.

We turned right towards the campsite, as we passed the park it was completely different from our last visit in winter, people were playing boules, others were in the five aside pitch, children were chasing balls while little dogs were chasing the children chasing the balls, parents sitting talking and eating at the stone tables, it was a lovely family affair.

We made a wide turn through the entrance of the campsite carefully avoiding the planted borders full of flowers that we had driven over the previous year, stopping at the reception we were greeted by Remy the owner and our local councillor, he was pleased to see us, we hadn't booked but he knew we were coming, news gets around.

He guided us to a hedge lined pitch with overhanging trees, thank goodness, we needed the shade it was in the top nineties, the campsite was full and lively, quite a contrast from last year. We unhitched the trailer and car, pulled the motorhome under a tree, before we could catch our breath we were descended upon by huge spiders abseiling down from the trees, little red insects with black spots seemed to leap onto every surface, large flying things with long dangly legs zoomed in on us, creatures of all shapes, sizes and colours must have thought a new playground had arrived. I was thinking about checking the bearing underneath the motor home but seeing the size of the ants running around I was afraid they might drag me off to some dark place and consume me, Sue shuddered as she looked around "Oh! They're big and creepy, I didn't expect this"

## Doubts and tears

We were both hot and tired but once settled and the shock wore off seeing our new campmates we made our way down to the mill just a short walk away, everyone we met said "Bonjour" it was catching and seemed very sincere.

As we approached the mill we couldn't believe our eyes, the once flat pasture was a huge jungle, in just seven months nature had overtaken time!

We had to fight our way through tall grass and nettles that towered above our heads as I trod a path towards the river, Sue following behind, suddenly she burst into a flood of tears and doubts "Are we doing the right thing" she asked, I consoled her, the vegetation beat us, some serious cutting equipment was needed, we turned around, made our way back to the campsite defeated, besides, we needed some food and rest after such a long journey.

We slept quite well considering the temperature. The morning after the event always seems a little more clear, Sue realised the fatigue from travelling down had fogged her judgment, yes, the land was overgrown, yes, there was a lot of building work but it's a new start in life, a new adventure. Cayriech was not remote or isolated, it had a community something that was sadly lacking back in England, it's for our retirement, a slower pace of life, something to be enjoyed, space to grow and tend the land.

Sue had missed her garden, our family house was set in a third of an acre on the edge of town, Sue had green fingers in abundance, growing melons and tomatoes in her greenhouse, outside were rows of flowers that she had dried and sold in her shop, her time spent on a horticultural course was put to good use, she had grown up with a garden, helping her dad, to grow and pick vegetables it was something that was done by most people in rural England, I, on the other had was lucky to see a window box being brought up in East London, a garden was a luxury

Our day was spent getting unpacked and set up for our long stay, in the evening we had a surprise visit, a couple from the next village, they had read my blog and popped through to introduce themselves, I got a little tipsy on a couple of glasses of Bordeaux, I'm not a big drinker, another glass and I would have been under the table, we had a pleasant evening's chat.

# Storms are brewing

Slowly melting in the heat ranging from 35 to 37 degrees, moving from motorhome with all fans at full blast, then to the safari room, then under the tree, and back again, we decided to call to see Remy our councillor and campsite owner, besides, the office had air-conditioning, he had arranged a visit to the DDE, the Director of council planning in a couple of days, whenever we mention the (pronounced) DiDee to any Frenchman we get raised eyebrows and a open fingered shake of the right hand and a deep intake of breath followed by aie! Do we need to worry? After a long chat with Remy pouring over the plans and perspectives that I had drawn up back in Barnsley of the mill, talking, albeit in pigeon French, we felt very positive, but then Remy seems to be on our side.

After living on salads since leaving the UK, I tried out my shiny new stainless steel drum barbeque, it was a big mistake, the heat generated from it could have melted gold, the chicken could have been used for deadly weapons, we ended up eating salad, Sue says if I carry on eating lettuce at this rate, I will grow long floppy ears to compliment my other rabbit affliction!

For a bit of relief we decided to have lunch at Saint Antonin, just 15 minutes away, trying to keep things safe we ordered what the locals were eating which turned out to be pretty tough steak burnt on the outside, raw on the inside, cold cauliflower, chips, and oh no! not more lettuce! Must remember not to order fruit juice again, we were plagued by kamikaze wasps that ended up drowning themselves in it. After lunch it was much too hot to look around the town so we returned to Cayriech, where we bumped into a fellow Yorkshireman who was down from Lyon where he lived, he was on a house-hunting trip and a holiday.

Remy had organised a camping get-together party night, he had been working away all day on the evening's menu, duck, potatoes, salad, desert, cheese, coffee, all washed down with wine & sangria, it was a good turnout, long tables were set out so that everyone could converse with each other, our French fellow campers were very friendly and welcoming, we hit it off with our new found friend from Lyon, after a drink or three we discovered we had the same sense of humour, imitating Peter Sellers (Inspector Clouseau) much to the amusement of everyone. Our new found friend, fluent and a translator in French, so, at least he could explain we were not poking fun at them.

Remy's father brought round some home made apple schnapps 65% proof, as I said before I am not a drinker but I did not want to offend their hospitality so I had some, one gulp had me doing an impression of the scene from Easy Rider where Jack Nicholson took a big swig of whiskey and said, "Nick..Nick..Nick" whilst moving his right elbow in time hitting the side of his chest as they sat around the camp fire, our French companions were rolling with laughter they must have seen the film! I felt my eyes roll as I gasped for a breath of oxygen.

A storm was brewing around Cayriech, the black clouds gathered, the wind got up, we heard thunder and thought it might spoil the evening but no, we seem to be in a little oasis, the jollity and laughter was suddenly broken by screams and chairs flying as the guests at one of the tables took flight, somehow from the sky a huge black insect as big as a hand had landed on the table moving slowly and looking like it was ready to jump in any direction, it seems everything from the insect world is on steroids, a Frenchman asked me to take it back to England, which got a round of laughter, a very brave soul transported it to a far off hedge to save the party. The evening was a great success, we felt very full with wonderful emotions.

Another very hot day 37deg in the motorhome again, we got off early to do some sightseeing at Saint Antonin, with the roof down on Sue's sports car, heading away from Septfonds, a short distance from Cayriech, travelling on the straight Roman roads that go on as far as the eye can see, then turning right towards Saint Antonin another perfectly straight Roman road climbs to a plateau before plunging into the Ayveron Gorge, flanked by the magnificent grey granite vertical cliffs as you wind down to the town with its terracotta roofed buildings and the river below. A very pretty medieval Town popular with British residents, we were told. Parking up we ventured into the small backstreets each building so close you could wash your neighbours windows. The church had wonderful stain glass windows, inside very cool and serene, as we wandered around it was strange to see 21st century people living in these old houses, how they had survived and what stories they could tell, my head filled with unanswered thoughts.

Having a cool drink in the square, taking in the atmosphere, watching the tourists wander around with their cameras, we could hear the chatter of some British diners and obvious residents, I named one Patsy (an Absolutely Fabulous Joanna Lumley lookalike) complete with fag and blond hair up, probably in her early 50's she was wearing a white jumpsuit, arriving on her cycle that had a little wicker basket on the front, I love me, love! It certainly amused us.

After exploring the town we returned to Cayriech for a very late lunch, our time clocks are all over the place. We decided to get dressed up for the first time since being in France and go out for a drive and a wander in Caussade and Puylaroque, it was a lovely warm evening for window shopping and people watching, it gave us time to note what shops we had in the town.

Returning later to the campsite it was refreshing to sit and chat to Remy, his wife and a couple from Switzerland, the language barrier didn't matter we all got on very well being able to understand and string the odd words together for basic chit chat...I think the way forward is not to be afraid of making mistakes and just go for it, Sue does most of the French reading.

The seemingly long wait for the DDE visit got off to a great start, Remy had a Swiss French speaking friend to interpret for us, we followed Remy to Caussade, at the office things seem to be on our side, the director of planning just happened to be our neighbour in Cayriech, he had played at our mill, swimming in the pools as a boy. Forearmed with construction books in French & English, CAD drawings and a lot of pre reading helped the meeting to go without a hitch and our project would able to proceed within guidelines and planning confirmation. The ancient mill, an integral part of the village and close to the church needed to reflect the architecture of the village when it's re-built. We have to consider the flood zone we are told, but before we flood the rest of the village would be well under water. Planning rules can be a little odd at times, anyway I will have a small rowing boat for messing about in and scuba gear if all else fails!

There is a threat of another storm which is brewing to the west, we have battened down the hatches trimmed the mainsail but it seems to be passing us by again here in Cayriech. We relax again and wait for forthcoming meetings, for anyone about to tread this long journey of French house purchase, at times your life seems to be on hold, waiting for that phone call, visit, or meeting it all takes "French" time and time has no meaning to some people so you have to accept it or it will drive you crazy! It's how France works, and it's how France has kept its charm!

The British and Dutch staying at the campsite are extremely inquisitive when they hear what we are doing, the comments range from Oh! What a big job! Aren't you worried with all the different ways of building in France! It looks a daunting task, good luck with an air of impending failure for us in their voice, or, "we couldn't do it, too much stress", and so on. I suppose they may look at my stature, I'm not a big burley type. The French say things Like Beaucoup de travaille, Bonne Chance or Bon Courage! As they shake their right hand with open fingers.

They don't know me!

I am a little fighter, I had to be! From birth at the beginning of the fifties I was diagnosed and looked upon as a sickly child, for the first seventeen years of my life I was being poisoned on a daily basis without anyone knowing including the many Doctors that had examined me.

Eventually Eureka!

I had Coeliac disease an auto immune system dysfunction, I was allergic to gluten, and for the last seventeen years I had been poisoned and had poisoned myself, resulting in malnutrition, causing essential vitamins and minerals just to pass straight through me and in turn starving my brain.

So when I am asked or questioned about, " do you think you can do it" "how do you cope" "how do you find the energy and strength to do whatever"! I remember the hard times, the sometimes very sad times, inner strength and determination, not to be beaten never taking no for an answer is my strength.

YES! Is the answer! Next question?

# New month, new beginning

The threatened storm eventually arrived late in the evening, I say storm it was more like a hurricane, anything that wasn't nailed down took flight, the rain was deafening as it pounded the motorhome roof, the paths outside were little rivers, lightning turned the night into day, the thunder sent vibrations through our bodies as we jumped into the air. We both put our heads under the covers to try and escape, but the storm was right over us, the thunder rattling the cups in the cupboards, we were in for a very long night. Somehow we drifted off to sleep!

August had arrived with a bang! the morning air was lighter, our body clocks are completely out of sync with everyone else's, by the time we have finished breakfast cleared up, which is very important when living in a relatively small space, it seems everyone on the campsite and in town are sitting down for lunch!

We just had to get into gear, deciding to do some early morning shopping in Caussade, returning to put our shopping away then relaxing, before our meeting. We are doing a lot of relaxing at the moment, this is unusual for us, we lead very busy lives back in the UK.

Returning to Caussade before lunch to meet Monsieur Larroque for our planned meeting with the Notaire. We were driven to Albias by Monsieur Larroque's partner leaving the three of us at the office as he had other appointments, we were shown into the Notaire's office, they had kindly arranged an interpreter for us to go through the stack of paperwork that had to be signed and counter signed which seemed endless.

Halfway through the Notaire stopped, looked up at Sue and said "Vous aimez de poisson" ? Sue replied "oui" I was completely in the dark what was happening. With her reply, the Notaire telephoned someone, finishing the call everyone stood up scraping their chairs backwards Monsieur Larroque looked at Sue and said in broken English "Its important to it" (eat) it was close to two o-clock, way past lunchtime. We were surprised but followed their lead and got off our chairs.

We were led out of the office and to the next block of buildings to a lovely Basque restaurant, it was closed but the owner, waiting by the door, unlocked it and beckoned us all in. The Notaire it seems is a very important man after all!

We were shown to a big round table, it was ready for a luncheon, in the middle of the restaurant there was a long open barbeque with oak logs crackling and spitting away, white hot embers lined the bottom, the chef was busy operating the large ancient leather bellows keeping the fire burning.

The griddle was laden with big chunks of pure white fish on long skewers, alongside even more skewers were filled with different coloured peppers, onions and large mushrooms. The mixture of aromas filled the air, salivating with apprehension, we were in for a feast, If that wasn't enough, the kitchen door opened and waiters carrying several large bowls of hot steaming haricots verts, proudly placing them on our table, then serving us several full skewers of the fish and mixed peppers on our plates with a "Bon appétit"

As we finished the main meal, the waiters appeared again carrying large plates of colourful chunky mixed salad, the contrast of smells from the cucumber, tomatoes, lettuce and coriander had that just-picked freshness smell. We felt very special.

After the meal and general chit chat we returned to the office, full and content with smiles on our faces.
We were feeling very relaxed for the final part of the paperwork marathon. The Notaire spoke to the interpreter, she then turned to me and said I had to write as she dictated on one of the prepared documents, suddenly I felt the back of my neck burning with heat, I struggled to stop my hand from shaking and I tried desperately not to glance at all the eyes

looking in my direction. The situation was out of my control I couldn't cover up my dyslexia, I went to pieces.

Sue stood over me almost spelling every word and letter, my writing looked like a three year old's work. If I had a shovel I would have dug a big hole and climbed in.

We finished off the rest of the signing, the time now way beyond British banking hours, it wasn't a problem we were told the transfer of our final payment could be done tomorrow and I could call back for the completed documents, after the weekend.

We, me and Sue, looked at each other puzzled, how do we get back to Caussade and our car? No problem, the Notaire was taking us. Outside he was busy emptying his car seats that were full of files and paperwork, stacking them in the boot together with other piles of paperwork, brief cases and general office stuff. He seemed to be enjoying himself cleaning out his car probably for the first time in a long time judging by the collection.

Delivering all three of us to Monsieur Larroques office we gave them both our warmest thanks and left in our car.

The river Le're that circles our land on three sides

On our way back to Cayriech we stopped for some shopping which included a rather expensive bottle of champagne (this is the first bottle we have ever bought in over 33 years of marriage)

We were able to finally go onto the land without feeling like trespassers. It was still too hot to tackle the six foot high grass, nettles, elderflower, thistles and other creeping stinging thingy's during the hottest part of the day, so we had a cycle around the area along the river bank. We had a look at another mill under construction further downstream. The abundance of wildlife is truly amazing, on the slow moving river we saw eight big water rats grazing away on the lily pads with their white noses dipping into the water, we were just feet from them and they didn't even give us a passing glance then in the next moment a 2 foot carp cruised past, no! It was more like 3 foot (sorry it's a fisherman thing) birds and exotic insects flying and crawling around, we just hope they don't bite.

We returned to the campsite later, loaded the car with cutting and strimming gear just as it was starting to cool down. At 8pm we drove to the mill, taking less than a minute, the sign at the gate says private property, but not for us, we climbed over, looked at the growth before us, after an hour's hard graft we had made a clearing, we decided to call it a night, we are so close to the village we didn't want to spoil anyone's evening with the noise from the strimmer.

Sunday, I was up with the Larks, the bit between my teeth, I was raring to go, hurried my breakfast down, loaded up my bike and rucksack and cycled off to the mill. It was a little early to start with the noisy brush cutter so I had a wander around the land and onto the river that is on three sides. I walked onto the weir looking up river for any movement of fish, frogs of various colours were hopping around avoiding my approach.

I then looked down river, it drops down several falls, the sound of the cascading water soothing but flowing with energy at the same time, just then, a kingfisher flew upriver towards me then darted away before disappearing into the overgrown wood at the back of the mill, it's been a while since I saw a kingfisher, we had one that visited our pond back in Barnsley, it would sit at the top of our small waterfall, diving in, a fishing expert, every time he would come out with a tiddler in it's beak holding it by its tail, then smacked the fishes head against a rock before tilting his head back and wiggled it down his throat, some things just make you smile.

I got a sweat on by the time Sue arrived, I had a breather before cutting a couple of trees down, so that Sue could remove all the branches with our large hand croppers leaving me to cut the large trunks with the bow saw. A chain saw would have been easier but we had to draw the line somewhere, we had so much stuff to bring to France.

Our days are made up by trying to catch up to French time, relaxing and shopping. We are limiting our time at the mill, an hour or two of hard work when its cool is best for us, rather than an all day slog in the sun getting sweaty and tired.

The money now transferred from the UK direct to the Notaire, we were summoned to his office in Albias to collect a copy of the final document, we left his office, said goodbyes to everyone, looked at each other and thought, well this is it, we now officially own our little bit of France! Our big smiles lasted all the way back to Cayriech.

A wonderful find! We were using the internet to show where our Moulin was in France to my brother some years later and this picture popped up.

It's by a French artist J. Bergere (deceased ) picture courtesy of Monsieur Bernard Auriol   Les Petites Toulousaines

Jazz & Blues our beloved Siamese cats. They always want to be in the thick
of it. Blues is on the left a blue point, Jazz is a seal point they are brothers.

# New friends

We met up with another UK couple on the campsite that had arrived some days earlier, they have been travelling around France..... Guess what!.... House hunting.

The planned evening campsite get together meal every Wednesday had to be cancelled, the rain had finally hit Cayriech with a vengeance, so we invited our new friends to share a meal and drink with us as the cloudburst fell noisily above us.

Our new neighbours from Preston, Alan and Vivien, Alan was a retired property developer, Viv was a retired school teacher, we got on very well, they asked us if we had time to go to look at some property and land with them, we were getting to know the area quite well. "Of course". On y va!

Being in France is for making new Friends and taking time for life. We spent a couple of days with them, viewing land, an old mill that had five storeys, it had been spoilt, someone had tried to restore it and used a lot of concrete, what a mess.

Several days later Alan & Viv returned triumphant, they had bought a plot of land in Lalbenque about twenty five kilometres away in the National park, where they planned to build a new house.

French time clocks now fully working, a beautiful blue sky with white fluffy clouds, the sun beating down upon us. We were having breakfast outside when we were joined by a young Dutch couple who were also house hunting, we gave them our limited advice and who to contact for some land that was for sale close by, they left. It was almost lunchtime.

Our campsite neighbours were getting curious, difficult to disguise the fact that something was going on when you are dressed in jeans, big boots, hard hats, carrying all sorts of cutting gear, going off and returning with bits of vegetation stuck to you, after explaining to them they showed great interest wished us luck saying "Bon courage!" with all the hard work ahead of us. The French people here are so nice, the children are lovely and polite it is a pleasure to be here!

Later after returning from another hour or so of cutting though the overgrown jungle we made arrangements with Remy and his wife to join us for a drink, after all, Remy had played an important part in our plans to secure our little piece of France.

The cork popped loudly with overflowing bubbles, we toasted with champagne, it tasted rather nice. We had French lessons from Remy's wife on how to pronounce the local towns that we have been getting wrong for over ten month's, it was a nice evening, the conversation was a little limited, Remy's English is zero!

# Decision time!

The UK was beckoning, our two sons now in their late twenties rang our mobile phone, Nathan, the eldest was in need of vegetables. Rory said he is doing all the housework and Nathan is not helping, where have we gone wrong? We checked ferry prices, Wednesday looked like a good day, but first we had a couple of important things to sort out. The Mairie was only open a few hours on Wednesday for the whole of August so it was to be our last chance to sort the forms that we collected from the DDE, for our permis de construire application.

Packing up Wednesday morning was a humongous task, it was made more difficult by our French camping neighbours calling by to wish us bon voyage and to ask about the mill, but we are in France, we have to make time to "stand and stare"! Finally packed up by noon, it left us time to visit the Mairie, the stand-in secretary was very helpful and spoke a little English, she filled in the forms as far as she could, we had to alter the plans and post photos back to her from the UK.

I made one last visit to the mill just to check things were OK, walking across to the river it was very peaceful, I was thinking about the project in front of us, just then a small snake about a foot long swam directly towards me and disappeared into the undergrowth, I stood motionless, this was the first time I have ever seen one in the wild, it must be more omens! I then returned to the camp site, I was greeted by two lovely French girls who gave me my very first French kisses....oh! One was five the other eight years old, everyone was so nice we were overwhelmed, saying goodbye took us to mid afternoon, after the long goodbyes we drove out of the campsite waving to everyone as we left.

We called into Caussade to fill up with cheap fuel, and then headed north on the autoroute. Our plan was to get up to Orleans, get a few hours sleep, then get around Paris in the early hours to miss the rush, which we did, but it also meant that the traffic moves at formula one race speed around the ring road which includes 40 ton juggernauts, passing us with just inches to spare at times and motorbike riders on a death wish.

Our journey back to Yorkshire was fairly uneventful apart from a rigorous search of the motorhome and passports at Dunkirk no less than 3 times, on the ferry we saw the news and realised what was happening, Terrorists were being hunted in the UK. We stopped at the services on the M20 to sleep and wait for a midnight dash for the M25 and Dartford tunnel, another stop at Leicester forest east services, pay and display in a motorway services! for parking! What next? Another good reason for moving to France.

We finally got back to our rented house Friday morning at 06:30, we were greeted by Jazz and Blues, our beloved Siamese cats, we fussed over them for half an hour, they were pleased to see us!

We took them out on their leads, let them into the motor home, letting them climb over the trailer so they could discover all the different smells we had brought back from France, (it's a cat owner thing) which one day will be their new home.

Our two sons gave us big hugs, our eldest had grown a goatee beard, he looked like me when I was his age, our youngest son's girlfriend said hi, they all got off to work, leaving us to an empty house ready to tackle the washing!

It was cold and windy; "we're missing the sun already!" We went through the post that was piled high. Back to reality so soon......OOOh! To be back in France!

# Get away or go mad!

Since our last visit to France, I had finished converting two flats above Sue's tea room and we had moved in to save renting. Most of our belongings were still in boxes waiting for their final destination, France! It wasn't ideal but we also had outside space to park the motorhome until the next phase of rebuilding. It was handy having everything under one roof so to speak, but we weren't used to living in a small flat, I was busy building and Sue was very busy in her shop, we just had to get away or go mad!

Our planned lunchtime departure to our little bit of France had passed. Sue's tea room was very busy and regular customers had been coming in since Friday to wish us well and it just continued into Saturday. The last few days had flown by as we were so busy getting ready. The motorhome was packed to the gunnels, but even so, we were sure we would forget something.

Our two boys had come to see us off, especially as it would be Sue's birthday while we are away. We gave Rhona (who works for Sue and looks after the business when she's away) a goodbye cuddle and we were off!

Finally, we were heading south on the motorway although much later in the afternoon and it was dismal. The wind was howling and with horizontal torrential rain but it didn't bother us. We were on another adventure.....Ok, Ok....I know it's not to the deepest jungle in some far off land! But we were off to France and stopping off at Rocamadour en route to cross another place off our wish list.

The journey to Dover was rough from the wind and rain. Oh! I did have a senior moment as I somehow took a wrong turn and ended up going around in circles. One of those twilight driving moments

As we arrived at the ferry port early, we chanced our luck and tried to board an earlier ferry but the grumpy ticket woman said, "NO. But YES, if you give me forty pieces of silver extra." We declined as we were in no rush but we were told we had to exit the terminal and come back later. As we drove out we were stopped by a nice customs man who said, "We could park in the coach bay while we waited for our 4.15 am ferry." So we had a few hours rest before departing for Calais.

There was quite a swell running so the ferry was rolling. There was nothing for it - a hearty breakfast of scrambled eggs, bacon, tomatoes and fried potato, all washed down with a couple of cups of rosy lee. That sorts the men from the boys! It was our little indulgence, not the normal breakfast but it was delicious.

# An alarming time

We arrived in Calais - breakfast intact - we headed south for Paris. Our plan was to get a few kilometres under our belt before stopping for a long sleep. Well that was the plan. Getting tired, we stopped at what we thought was a quiet Aire. Just as we were getting ready for bed we heard an almighty roaring sound approaching. Cars, lorries and a herd of 20 Belgian bikers turned up. What a racket! It must have been a meeting place for a chinwag. We decided to find somewhere else. We were, by now, getting very tired but, thankfully, twenty kilometres further south we found a deserted Aire in a little wooded area.

One thing I like about France is that you can stop on a motorway Aire, spend all night there and you don't get a parking ticket, unlike the motorway services in the UK.

It was now 8am and our body clocks were all to cock. What with the different time zone and hence the clocks going forward and eating when we should be sleeping it was a topsy-turvy time.

We had bought a new Stressfree mattress, new bedding and fluffy duvet so we drew the blinds, pulled the curtains closed and I set the newly installed and modified burglar alarm system. (Only tested in laboratory conditions). The whole of the front area of the motorhome was protected from intruders while we slept. We got naked and climbed into bed. We cuddled but started giggling like a couple of teenagers and to think we had just celebrated our 35th wedding anniversary. We were at last relaxed and on holiday. Bonne nuit!

I woke at 4pm after a lovely refreshing and undisturbed sleep. I got up but I had not seen one of my new CAT boots – they are designed for protection and to ensure you are slip-free when I climb onto my CAT excavator – as it was lying next to the bed, It had welded itself to the vinyl floor and I tripped over it, stubbing my toe.

The remote for the alarm leapt from my outstretched hand, went flying forward and slid under the table. I rushed forward, ignoring the pain in my toe. As I did so I set the alarm off. With sirens wailing and lights flashing, I grabbed the remote from under the table but hit my head on the corner of the table on the way up. So there I was, naked, hopping about and holding my head, with flashing lights and blaring sirens and with my dangly bits moving in opposite directions. It was like a naked highland fling. Not a pretty sight, or so I was told by a now hysterical Sue.

We have now concluded that provided the burglar is naked….the alarm is fool-proof!

# Southward bound

Getting on our way, we made good time and hit the outskirts of Paris around 6 pm ready to join the kamikaze ring road. We needed our wits about us and kept a very sharp look out. The traffic was mad, weaving and joining, leaving from all directions, continuous lane changing, four lanes into two, then three and visa versa. Not for the novice driver. All was fine until we hit a wall of traffic half way round and from then on we crawled round to the south-side. During this time we had a few raised eyebrows, and some smiles, at our Hymer and the well laden trailer.

Finally we were heading out on the A10 and completely unscathed. We were making for a stop south of Orleans, a quiet Aire where we had stayed before. By now we were feeling tired from the journey, plus the weather was pretty grim and we needed food and sleep. Oh, I forgot to mention, in the middle of the night Sue woke me up to tell me she had left two packs of vine tomatoes in the cupboard back in Barnsley. So we were on green salads only. By the time we got to the Aire it was getting late so we had some supper before slumping into bed and going into a deep sleep.

It was a cold wet Monday morning. I got up and peered through the curtains. Only one other traveller parked up. It was very quiet considering we were adjacent to the autoroute. So nice not to be going to work. I put the heating on. Sue was still snuggled under the fluffy soft duvet and she wasn't getting out until it reached at least 80 degrees. I put the kettle on for a cup of tea. Harking back to my sail training days, I was always first up making the tea, driving everyone mad with the clanking of mugs and being cheerful. I still haven't changed. Every now and then Sue would shout out, "Shut up."

After we had showered and had breakfast I went outside to clean the windows before our departure. Whilst cleaning the passenger side closest to the woods I could here a chirping noise. I looked down at my feet and there was a finch chirping away as if to say, "Feed me. Feed me." I called to Sue through the window, "Pass me some bread quick." It wasn't just any old bread - cue the music - it was whole grain M&S bread! I pulled little bits off to feed it almost from my hand. The colourful, brave little finch had now been joined by a blue tit and even more finches. What a lovely start to our morning. It was one of those nice Oooooo feelings! After we got over the excitement we got on our way.

The wind that had followed us down from Yorkshire had died away but sporadic rain persisted. Our next goal was to head for Rocamadour and some sightseeing.

The journey south was pretty boring. Sue broke the monotony by trying to teach me to count in French. Ascending in numbers by counting how many lorries passed us going north. I glazed over when we reached 71 and things got a bit complicated.

In the misty, rain covered landscape we noticed an array of flashing strobe lights in the distance and as we got closer it was apparent that there was a huge construction programme of a wind farm. The turbines were towering into the sky. Huge cranes were lifting the sections of tubular supports. On one side of the landscape they were all flashing white strobes and on the other side they were all blinking red. There was so many you could probably have seen them from space.

We were now reaching the Limousin region. The tell tale sign is I have to drop down the gears to crawl up the hills. The 3ltr 5cyl Mercedes engine isn't renowned for its hill climbing abilities, but it was pulling over 5 tons. Thankfully, we were not in any rush.

We stopped for yet another green salad lunch. Gingerly I opened the overhead lockers that were jammed full with tins, jars and even spices for curries. A packet of popadoms had been leaping out of one of the cupboards for the last few days rather like a jack-in-the-box. It now resembled a packet of cornflakes. Still, it made a change from tins and jars.

We were also down to two bone china cups and four saucers - they don't bounce too well.

Lunch was finished so we headed even further south. We climbed hill after hill but on the horizon we could see a storm brewing. As we drew closer we could see sheets of rain falling in the distance. We were now dropping down a very long hill to the Vallée de Brive. Almost immediately we were pelted with hailstones followed by heavy rain as we descended . Once we were down in the valley the rain was so heavy the road was like a river. It would have been easier with a boat. It was a hell of a storm!

We decided to drive into Brive to do some tomato shopping. We had never been into Brive but I just followed my nose and we happened upon a Lidl. We picked up some fresh tomatoes, milk and water for the rest of our journey. We didn't stop for a look around as it was still very wet and it was now after 6 pm.

Making good progress we crossed into the Lot region. We joined the new section of the toll paying autoroute. The weather was still very bleak. Do we go to Rocamadour or continue south towards Cayriech? The clouds were very low. Going through one of the valleys we saw six wild deer grazing in the fields next to the autoroute. They merely glanced up at us as we passed. It's so nice to see wildlife – it's that Oooo feeling again!

We passed the junction for Rocamadour. I was disappointed, knowing that returning back to the UK in a few weeks, we would not have time for sightseeing. But visiting somewhere in this weather wouldn't be any fun, so we headed further south for the autoroute services, Jardin des Causses, where we had stayed before. We parked in the same spot overlooking the little valley with the church on the hillside. We anticipated being woken in the early hours by the truckers leaving because as usual the services were full. In fact we were lucky to find a space.

Our sleep pattern was still out of sync, added to the excitement of the days that lay ahead, it was not surprising that we were not feeling tired. I decided to get a bottle of wine from the services shop. Not realising it was getting so late I found the staff were doing stock checks and wouldn't serve me, so I returned back to the motorhome empty handed.

I searched through the lockers for the board games as I really did not want to be messing about fitting up the sat dish and watching the TV. Do we play forfeits? There were only two of us so it wouldn't take long to get to the parts where you have to remove bits of clothing. Besides you can't class a thong as a bit of clothing, can you? It had to come off anyway as it was cutting me in half.....only kidding! We decided on scrabble!

Now you have to understand that playing scrabble with me is a painful, slow process. Being dyslexic, I can't even remember how to spell it most times, my opponent has to be very patient. It was no mean feat that I was in the lead by nearly 10 points throughout the game and that's not easy with 3 letter words and an occasional 4 letter one. But it all changed by the last go. Yep! I had Q, V and X etc. What do you spell with them? Most of the time the letters look gibberish to me, but when you have seven of them in front of you. UGH! I lost. Sue had lulled me into a false sense of security. The time was now 1.30am and still very wet and overcast and we were still disappointed about missing Rocamadour. Maybe another year? Looks like an early start for Cayriech so we decided to go to bed.

Our slumber was disturbed at around 5am as expected. Half an hour later all was quiet again as the 40 or so trucks had left the services and we drifted back off to sleep.

# Do we or don't we?

Awoken by a bright beam of light shinning though the motorhome roof light I looked at the clock. It was 10am! So much for our early start for Cayriech. I tip-toed along the cold floor, made an eye-sized gap in the curtains and peered through. "Sun," I yelled. The first we had seen since leaving the UK. Well not quite bucket loads but broken cloud. I looked across the little valley. The deep lush green grass was highlighted with rays of sun making splashes of light green here and there. It all looked quite promising.

The heating was put on full blast, as I shivered putting on my freezing cold tracksuit bottoms and sweat shirt. I was stumbling around looking for some socks and trying unsuccessfully to avoid putting my feet on the cold vinyl floor. Sue was, as usual, curled up under the duvet - she's a fire sign. No way was she getting up in this cold. I put the kettle on for a cuppa!

After breakfast and a hot shower we felt revived from the cold morning. We drove round to the motorhome service bay to empty tanks and fill our now depleted fresh water tank. Whilst doing so, the sun was getting stronger, clouds were breaking up and giving way to a beautiful blue sky. The motorhome was acting as a wind break so we were in a little sun trap. I imagined how it must feel to be a reptile basking and waiting to warm up before it moves around. It was certainly welcome and therapeutic standing there slowly filling the tank in the sun. We looked at each other and said, "Rocamadour!"

Everything stowed away, trailer checked over, wheel straps on Sue's car intact and tight. I checked the map. Just a short way back northwards on the autoroute, out of the péage and through Germat. We have to pick our route carefully. On small roads hairpin bends on a hill climb can be very tricky for our 42 foot home and trailer on wheels.

Like most French roads it was a smooth and quiet run. We were making good progress when suddenly a huge bird of prey swooped across the road in front of us. What a sight! The wingspan was almost the size of our windscreen.

We were getting closer to Rocamadour with the sun brighter by the minute and clouds giving way to more blue sky. It was a very clean and tidy area. The houses and farms were well kept with rustic canal tiles in shades of browns, oranges and creams on the shallow pitch roofs, which were common to these areas, dotted about the undulating landscape and perched on little hillsides.

Relaxing in the evening sun in Cayriech, Camping le clos de la le're
Left to right  Steve, Susan, Peter & Eileen

# Panoramic magnifique!

We had arrived at the east side of Rocamadour, the Hospitalet town area. We saw a campsite on our right and pulled in. We were at an altitude on what seemed to be a plateau. We couldn't work out where a hill would be with the houses on. We were a little confused.

We booked into reception. There were only four or so other camper vans on the site that could easily accommodate more than 50. The owner showed us to our bay. We unhitched the trailer, parked the motorhome and then had a late lunch.

Lunch over, we called into the campsite reception to pick up a map and advice of where everything was. The young lady spoke no English but I understood remarkably well. Thanking her in my best Inspector Clouseau accent we walked across to a viewing point. Easily spotted by the big telescope concreted into the floor – It's always a giveaway.

We looked out across the deep gorge. It was a jaw dropping moment. The description given to us by a French couple, fellow Hymer motorhomers we had met a couple of years ago in Cahors, of "Panoramic magnifique" lived up to and beyond our expectations. Buildings of all shapes and sizes were clinging to the side of a sheer cliff. Huge overhangs of rock above giving shelter to the buildings underneath almost defying gravity. A château perched on the top, a church to one side with archways and tunnels leading to the base of the labyrinth. The sunlight was casting shadows over the buildings creating depth to this beautiful creation. After the shock of this truly magnificent construction we eagerly made our way down to the village.

We went through a little arch from the Hospitalet area, and down a steep single track road lined on one side with tiny white stone houses, built into the rock face, and little well-kept gardens opposite on the other side of the track, filled with flowers in full bloom, the scent carried on the breeze.

We carried our sweat shirts but there was no need of them. We were sheltered from the cool breeze and our bodies embraced the welcome rays of the sun. It was out of season, so we were told, hence very quiet. There was just one coach-load of elderly Irish Catholic pilgrims. It seemed that each family had brought their own priest. That was quite a sight too.

We entered the tiny main street through the Porte de Figuier archway. It was obvious a lot of restoration work had been done and it was very sympathetic. The once little houses are now shops of all descriptions and fitted to a very high standard. Yes, there were plenty of souvenir shops but this was outweighed by the architecture of the buildings. Our jaws were constantly dropping, our necks cricking as we gazed up high to the overhanging cliff and the buildings that seem to have been welded to its face. Almost too much to take in. We climbed the steep wide steps that reach up to the Sanctuaries, passing a couple of elderly pilgrims. They were out of breath and too frail so they were turning to go back down and use the cable car. The climb was too much for them. The worn solid stone steps revealed that they were encrusted with sea fossils.

Reaching the holy churches wasn't a step but a leap back into the past. It was very quiet and surreal. The only sound was of birds chirping, wings flapping and our own footsteps echoing and bouncing off the stone walls with their many doors, arches and stone staircases. Looking up at a very ornate stone balcony that followed the curved building on one side, you could just imagine a fair maiden calling to be rescued, or Errol Flynn, sword in hand, fighting off the baddies.

What a place. Inside the dark old buildings it was very cool and at times a chill rushed my spine. It was getting late so we made our way further up to the château. We used the cable car that runs inside the stone cliff through a very steep tunnel. Reaching the top we were in the sun again. We made our way to the coffee shop where we sat and contemplated while drinking cappuccino.

Arriving back at the campsite we realised several hours had flown by. There was too much to see, we decided to stay overnight and explore even further tomorrow.

We had a late breakfast giving the sun plenty of time to wake up and warm the stone buildings. As we passed by the only other motorhome on the campsite, we said our cheery hellos to the occupants and made our way once again to the viewing point. We stood and stared, the views were breathtaking. We meandered our way down to the village, calling into one or two shops on the way and talking to the shopkeepers, who were very friendly and polite. There were no coaches today so it was even quieter. We explored every nook and cranny, going through doors, looking in the dark, cool churches where the stained glass windows were strategically placed to catch the sun. Stepping out onto the cobbled courtyard the warmth of the sun wrapped itself around us, we looked up towards the roof tops, marvelling at the ornate buildings, this was the old Rocamadour.

This time we used the steep winding track to reach the château. On every bend there was a praying place. A stone arched monument with figures. One depicted Jesus carrying the cross and below was an inscription. Each one was different and as they ascended to the top of the climb it took you through the life of Jesus. There were unfinished caves and viewing points. You could see over the roofs of the buildings below and views over the gorge across to the manicured green valley with its little winding river. There was so much to take in.

Many of the attractions and shops were not opening until the 5th April – not yet the true tourist season! We headed back to the campsite, calling at the grocers on the way for some salad produce.

Saying hello to a fellow motorhomer again as we passed by, he called us back for a chat. He and his family were from Norway. They were on an 8 week holiday driving down to relatives who lived in SE France. During their journey they had been stuck in snowdrifts for several days in Sweden and Germany and were glad to see some sun. They were a lovely family, him and his wife with two young boys the eldest being four. They insisted that we had some Norwegian coffee. Out came an old copper and brass kettle which he placed on the gas stove. With the water warming, he opened a new packet of ground Norwegian coffee and put some into the kettle. Once it had boiled he lifted it off the stove and with an out-stretched arm, he raised the kettle above head height and down again several times. Was it a ritual? No, it was the Norwegian way to mix the water and coffee. Very special for the flavour he told us. He was quite a comedian and had us laughing most of the time. We exchanged telephone numbers and email addresses and they asked if they could visit us at Cayriech later in April on their way back to Norway. We waved them goodbye as they left.

We returned to our motorhome, made ready, hitched up the trailer and car and said our goodbyes to the campsite owners. The wonderful thing about travelling around is you meet such lovely people. We drove out of the campsite. It was early afternoon with the sun shining bright and warm. Cayriech was only an hour away. We were getting both excited and apprehensive as there had been a lot of heavy rain during March. How had the river around our mill coped? We shall soon see. Next stop Le Landes Moulin, Cayriech - our little bit of France.

# The anticipation is excruciating.

Getting over the excitement of the magnifique Rocamadour, we joined the new autoroute southwards. The sun was shining bright in clear blue skies. The landscape changed as we entered, the now familiar, Tarn-et-Garonne. We drove through the tunnels and as we emerged each time the light seemed to become brighter and clearer. Amazing panoramic views together with trees and birds of all shapes and sizes. I shouted to Sue, "Cor, look at that one!" as we passed yet another large bird of prey sitting on a fence, probably waiting for some road kill. There was a hovering kestrel and then we saw a heron stalking its prey in a field. Lucky this major road is pretty quiet as there is so much to look at. Although, when I was a kid my mum, in her cockney accent, used to say to me, "You've got eyes in the back of your head" as I never missed a thing.

We pass the historic pigeonnier, next to the autoroute, on the outskirts of Montpezat de Quercy. It's a protected heritage building depicted on numerous posters and cards. Sad that the autoroute passes so close but that's progress for you. We start to get closer to Caussade, our turn off point with the landscape taking on a more Mediterranean feel. This last leg of our journey is extremely relaxing but our feelings are running high with excitement at the same time.

We leave the autoroute, pay our dues at the péage and head for Caussade town centre. The first thing we notice is that we have a new Lidl. Driving on we leave the commercial area and enter the town. We have a big advantage sitting high up in the motorhome cab as our eyes pan from side to side. The town is so inviting with trees either side of the road, planters with evergreens creating parking areas, ornate wrought iron dividers, cafés with seating outside on the pavement, people sitting eating, drinking and chatting…all very relaxed. We are just over a couple of hours from the Mediterranean and it shows. We drive through the centre, our motorhome and car in tow, causes many a glance in our direction.

Once through Caussade, we pass through Monteils, a residential area with a tree lined small main road. It has low level buildings with colourful canal tiled rooftops, window boxes and neat gardens in full bloom even though it's only just April. There are familiar faces playing boules, as usual, and a new cleaned up parking and picnic area next to the very well kept stone walled cemetery.

Cayriech is only minutes away now. We drive over the bridge which crosses a small river that joins the Le're - this is the river that runs around our land - we're getting closer! The anticipation is excruciating! The road is lined with towering plane trees, with their pale olive smooth bark with dark and light patches like camouflage. These trees grow very large and they line the road on either side in several places towards Cayriech. In full leaf they create a huge cathedral arch where they touch. So very French!

As we pass the houses here and there we take note of who has done some improvements, who has finished - or not. We pass a house on our left which always makes us laugh as it is called Le Tourniquet. We can only presume he is saddled with a huge mortgage. We approach the last sweeping right hand bend, the last leg of our journey on the smooth almost traffic free roads as we reach the turning for Cayriech.

Driving down the lane which is just wide enough for two cars, our eyes are acting like telescopes looking into the valley. The dark and light green fields creating a patchwork quilt. "Can you see the church yet"? I ask. Nothing had changed much except for a couple of new properties on the new residential site which is set aside above the flood zone. Just bungalows, all different designs, all rendered, one painted pastel blue, others in shades of cream and all with colourful canal tiles.

Getting closer the road now drops down to the medieval village. As we pass the last crossroad before the humpback bridge we look to our left. "Can you see our land?" I ask.

We cross over the river Le're, driving slowly while trying to see how full it is. "It doesn't look too bad," I say. On our left is the beautiful restored church with its colombage design. On we go to the lovely clean little street. God it feels like coming home! A house on our right that had been hit by a freak storm has been repaired and was looking like new. We get to the T junction and turn right. Now we can see the campsite. We cross over to the other side of the little road and make a wide sweep into the entrance - carefully avoiding the neatly manicured flower borders full of brightly coloured pansies that we flattened one dark night on our first visit with our car transporter.

It's very quiet. There's no one about, no other campers or motorhomes. We drive to the reception and to where we had pitched before. Just then we see Remy the campsite owner and our village councillor. We stop and get out and we greet each other with the usual cheerful "Bonjour" and hearty handshake. He kisses Sue on either cheek. It was a happy and sad moment. I lent forward and hugged Remy. I whispered in his ear, "Je regret pour Mark." Our eyes welled with tears. Nothing more could be said for a few moments. His son, 21 years old, had died in tragic circumstances. Last September we were telephoned back in the UK with the sad news. Also Remy's father had died the month before. It had been an extremely difficult time for the family.

Looking into each other's eyes, I did not have to imagine, I saw and felt the pain he was still going through. My younger baby brother Dene, died at the age of two. He had survived his twin sister Deon, she had died earlier in hospital due to hospital negligence. I was fourteen at the time. My mother divorced when I was 10, so we were on our own.

At home on that fateful day the police knocked on our door, they had come to take us to the Hackney children's hospital where Dene was having tests for Leukaemia. Mum managed to get a neighbour to look after my other brother, while we were driven to the hospital. We were in a panic when we arrived. In the Doctors office, we were told that Dene had fallen from the 4th storey window of the hospital to his death. The horrific news hit us hard. I cannot put into words what my mum and I went through but I never want to hear screams like that again. The later post mortem, and the tests he had had, showed there was nothing wrong with him. During the following months I found, and stopped, my mother trying to commit suicide on a few occasions. We all lived in the, then slums of Bethnal Green. We had just two rented rooms. It was tough!

The sad moment had passed for both of us.

Remy said in French (his English is worse than my French) that we had to park at the transit end as the camping area was too waterlogged. By this time Remy's wife and daughter had come out to say "Bonjour." Sue had a quiet word with Jocelyne, Remy's wife.

A common sight in French villages, a cat keeping watch over it's territory.

# Friendly surprise

We slowly reversed and turned around the tight corner with the trailer still attached. Good job I've had plenty of practice. We then made our way to the other end of the camp to the hard standing and motorhome service area.

The sun was burning bright and very warm in a cloudless blue sky. The limestone gravel reflected in the sun. It was paradise but a slight breeze now and again brought with it a little chill - well it was only just April!

We parked up in the middle, left the motorhome with trailer and car attached. Well we did have the campsite to ourselves so that wasn't a problem. Remy was busying himself with work as usual. We put on our walking boots. Sue called out to Remy, "Nous allons au Moulin." We walked briskly out of the campsite suppressing the urge to break into a run. The suspense was killing us. Our mill (ruin) was just a couple of minutes away on the other side of the village.

As expected the village was clean and tidy with flowers everywhere, gardens and tubs overflowing. Everyone in the village had a reputation to uphold as winners of the Concours European de L'Entente Florale 2004.

A big black dog that lives in the corner house barked as we passed.
Comme d'habitude. We were then greeted by noisy geese alerting the house owners that someone strange was close by, chickens clucking

running around in a panic. A beautiful cockerel stood tall and proud and a peacock on seeing us started to display. His feathers outstretched and his breast an iridescent purple/turquoise. It was so quiet - other than the wildlife. We called "bonjour" to a neighbour as we turned up the track leading to our mill and grange.

As we approached our eyes scoured one of our fields. We could now see the many fruit trees that had been planted. This was not possible during our last visit as the vegetation had been over 6 foot high.

Nothing much seemed to have changed since our last visit. As we drew closer, a big light tan and white owl flew out of our grange. The magpies and other birds swooped at it, chattering and complaining as it flew high into the trees. We got closer to the wire gate fence, the "Private" sticker still intact. We could hear the river for the first time with the sound of rushing water flowing over the weir but still only imagining not seeing. I hurriedly helped Sue through and over the gap.

Now it was my turn. Eagerly wanting to actually see the river, I misjudged the opening. One leg through and foot firmly on the ground but my other leg, on its way, caught the wire. I fell backwards, giving a yell and laughing on the way down, with one foot still stuck on the wire. I lay sprawled in a bed of nettles. At least it was a soft landing.

We walked over our little canal bridge, up the sloping grass banking and over to the river. The sound of rushing water increasing with every step then what a sight! Water cascading over the waterfalls, crystal clear, white rapids, swirling eddies, oxygen bubbles and so much energy. It was quite hot, 20°, but we had a lovely fresh breeze from the spray.

I had forgotten my camera in the rush. I told Sue I was going back for it and to wait by the river. I walked, ran, trotted, hopped and tripped over the nettles and brambles. Half running through the village, using a back street shortcut, and clomping loudly in my walking boots as I went, I hastily looked around in case the villagers wondered who this demented Englishman was running in the hot sun. Why was I running? The river wasn't suddenly going to stop but you try telling that to a demented Englishman on a mission!

As I reached the gate to the camping site I was greeted by Peter & Eileen from Lancashire. They had driven up from Spain to see us and they had arrived a few days early just to surprise us. They had been away since last September wintering, as they do every year, in Spain in their motorhome. After hugs, I sent Eileen down to the mill to surprise Sue while Peter walked with me to get my camera.

After returning to the mill, taking some photos and having a good catch-up chin wag we all returned to the campsite for tea. We met up later in the evening in our motorhome for an even longer chat. After a glass of red I performed a re-enactment of the highland fling episode - fully clothed though. We don't know them that well!

It's home, our little oasis. Rose tinted specs or not we will take things as they come - good or bad!

Village houses Cayriech. Typical architecture of the Tarn-et-Garonne

# Unexpected changes

A very chilly night - minus four degrees. Waking several times from the cold I put the central heating on, including the electric halogen rad. This end of Cayriech is always cooler than the other. It was 5am and I'm now wide awake and my mind working overtime. I made a cuppa, trying very carefully not to make any noise, but being afflicted with dropsy anyway. First the cup, then the lid off the tea jar followed by the spoon. "Shut up," Sue called out. "What time is it?"......"Oh, about 6am," I fibbed. The heat was filtering through to the back bedroom and Sue drifted back off to sleep. By the time the clock said 6am, I had had two cups of tea, a bowl of crunchy nut cornflakes, a grapefruit and a packet of gluten free shortbreads.

I switch the laptop on and tapped away on the keyboard – quietly. Thoughts and vivid pictures were flooding out faster than I could type. I occasionally peered through the curtains to see what was going on outside. The sun was rising, the early frost melting fast, a cuckoo was calling and another strange bird sound - it had been calling for most of the night with a single hoo! The call filling in the gaps left by the cuckoo were short and evenly spaced. We have a lot to discover.

By 9 o'clock the sun was shining brightly through the side window. I looked out at the donkey in the field. Braying with its head over the fence and looking at me. It's got sad eyes I thought. I throw caution to the wind and I get a hot shower. Sue knocks on the wall and hollers, "can't you ever be quiet, what time is it?"

I prepare a second breakfast for us both. Like a greyhound in the trap waiting for the hare to pass I am itching to get down to the mill. I am always seven jumps ahead of myself.

Sue was finally ready so we made our way to the mill. On our way we call in to see Remy and his family, we had brought them a little present from the UK - a large presentation tin of M & S Scottish shortbread biscuits. We had a chat and were surprised to hear that he was no longer a councillor. But further shocked that our lovely mayoress had also gone. Cayriech, amongst other communes, was going through centralisation. Sarkozey wielding his sword of cuts and changes.

We continue our walk with camera in hand this time. As we approach the owl takes flight from the eaves of our grange, swooping high into the trees. Once again the other birds complain loudly. Magpies and various tiny birds dart about. We are causing a disruption in this tranquil place.

The river is still running fast and in fact, higher than we have ever seen it. It's like a distorted magnifying glass in the places where it passes over the rapids and clearly showing the rock below. Spray sparkled in the morning sun. I had originally wanted to buy a place next to the sea but it wasn't practical, or affordable, and besides it gets so busy with tourists and day trippers. Thankfully, we have stumbled upon a gem of a place and, like the sea, the river can change daily. On top of that we have the added bonus of peace and quiet.

# All about Pooh!

We walked almost every inch of our land, following the path around the river, jumping across the canal to our other field where most of the fruit trees are. We have a hazel and walnut trees behind the mill. We have found shells buried by an animal.

We discuss where the fosse septique would go but this will be decided tomorrow when we have a site meeting with SPANC, previously arranged back in the UK.

We returned to the campsite. The warm bright sunshine is so welcome after our very wet journey south. We set up the awning and the safari room, fitting up tables and chairs for a leisurely lunch with Peter and Eileen.

The meeting went very well with SPANC but it brought home to us just how little French we know. The young lady didn't speak any English and she rattled along at tremendous speed. Thankfully, we had a common understanding of plans and technical terms, otherwise it would have been a complete waste of time. Luckily Sue had been studying a lot with her French teacher so she helped by filling in my blanks. We had several options agreed upon and I was to make further contact when I was ready to start excavating.

Two ladies that lived in the Moulin picture taken 1944
The Moulin in the background is in better condition than today

Photograph courtesy of Cayriech Maire

## Lost in more ways than one

The sun getting stronger by the day, we decided to walk along the lanes next to the river and around Cayriech, chatting to folk that we passed. We reached the next mill on the river below ours. It has been under reconstruction for the last 5 years and not a lot had changed since our last visit. Talking to a farmer nearby, I got the complete wrong end of the stick. I thought he said that the mill owner had died. We later found out he's a bit lazy. I say, "Je dois" - "I must" learn more French!

We Join Peter and Eileen for a sightseeing trip to Montauban in their motorhome. Montauban is a large town about 20 mins away. It's fantastic for commerce but it was very busy so not my cup of tea. We found our way to the Place Royale, a square in the old town. It has some very impressive architecture. None of the internal corners met at 90° but are joined at 45° with an arched entrance at all four points. The building has impressive multiple arches on all ground floor elevations that join and radiate inwards, increasing in size, then the areas that are now shops have huge cathedral ceilings. It's all very complex and built in red handmade clay brick.

The square is used for a market and café seating. It was a warm sunny day and lunch time approached so we decided to sit at one of the many tables. I needed to use the loo in the café. I could not believe my eyes, nor my nose when I went in. The toilet, well I wont go into too much detail, just imagine the worst. It was right next to the kitchen and the chap before me walked straight out, didn't wash his hands, went into the kitchen and started serving. I peered into the kitchen. YUK. I walked out to the others who were just about to place their order. I said, "We are leaving." A startled waitress tried to call us back. Not likely!

We carried on and explored the many little streets and courtyards that radiated outwards. Well worth a visit. Then, in complete contrast, we went to Geant Casino, a huge modern shopping area. Again, not my cup of tea, but we decided to get some lunch at the cafeteria. Eileen piped up, "I've lost my spectacles." Yep! She had left them at the table at the dodgy toilet café when we made our hasty exit.

Peter and I drove back while Sue and Eileen did some shopping. Our plan was to park as close to the square as possible and Peter, who speaks French, (in a fashion), would try to recover the specs. So far so good. Nowhere to park, of course. So I take over and plan to drive round in circles in the one way bit around the car park. But the barrier is too low to take a motorhome. So Peter jumps out with my passing words, "Don't get lost. Remember that dirty great white building over there!"

It was during my tenth circuit with cars sounding their horns that I noticed I was getting some funny looks and the lady in the shop watching the commotion was unscrewing her neck. I also noticed that I was getting the evil eye from the Gendarmes. Around the 12th circuit, I saw, with some relief, Peter appearing from around a corner, his arm was raised with Eileen's glasses in his hand. He came from completely the wrong direction. Yes he had got lost!

Eventually we arrived back at the shopping complex for some very late lunch. It was bedlam, talk about frying pan and fire, children running around everywhere and the noise was deafening. It seemed ok to Peter and Eileen they had been there many times before so perhaps they knew what to expect. I whispered to Sue, "Next time we take our hiking hamper and our own food." She nodded in agreement. Yet another eventful day.

# Damp, but not our spirits

Next morning was overcast so we decided to go to the Sunday Market in St Antonin Noble Vale with Peter and Eileen. It's fifteen minutes from Cayriech and during our last visit I saw Patsy (Joanna Lumley) of Absolutely Fabulous. Well her double actually, she was wearing a white jump suit, fag hanging out of her mouth, riding her bicycle and then stopped at a bar. She was so - OK, look at me darlings!

This time we saw Max Headroom! He was quite tall, bleached and highlighted swept back hair, bright red designer glasses that you noticed before him. He was in his mid 50's and he was out to be seen by parading up and down. There are quite a lot of Brits in this area.

We bought some produce, wine, some odds and ends and went exploring the many interesting back streets with beautiful medieval buildings. The town square is the centre piece with its big stone pillars and granite steps and surrounded by colombage buildings, some of which overhang the street.

It was quite busy in the narrow streets with the market stalls placed either side. There's a real diverse variety of stalls selling home made wines, local produce and bread, as well as the usual tourist stuff. We then called to the hot chicken stall with it's vertical multiple rotisserie. Rows of chickens, ducks and little birds, all complete with heads that looked at you and then flopped over when they went round. We chose a nice plump roast chicken and took it back to Peter and Eileen's motorhome where we had a feast. We arrived back at the campsite to a lovely relaxing sunny afternoon.

The next few days the weather was changeable. The surrounding hills had dark clouds over them but our little pocket of sun in the centre enabled us to do a little work on the land. In between bouts of work we contemplated, dreamed and discussed our plans.

It was hot and humid, the hottest day so far, but we could see, and hear, a storm brewing in the distance. There was fork lightning. Will it miss us again, leaving us with sun? Later in the afternoon, and suddenly, like switching on a big fan, the wind blew up, then, a sound like huge trucks fast approaching. The storm went straight through us. The awning roof parted company with the safari room. With outstretched arms I clung to it but the force was almost lifting all 10 stone of me off the ground. I imagined myself being carried off feet first into the sky and disappearing into the eye of the storm like in some storm-chaser film. Although I had been ready for it and had tied it down with guy ropes, the roof clips just pulled away. Somehow in the rain and wind I managed to fit the whole thing back together. Just then I was hit on the head with huge hailstones. I ran inside to take cover. The stones were bouncing off Sue's car. "Will they damage it?" I shout. The noise is deafening on the motorhome roof and the ground was now covered with white ice balls. All this was followed by heavy rain. The storm continued north and it had passed as quickly as it had arrived.

I sent a quick text to a friend saying "a storm is coming your way." I knew they were putting the roof on their new house about 20km further north. We later learned that the roofers had fled the site but thankfully all was OK.

We had torrential heavy rain all night long, keeping us awake as it pounded noisily on the roof. I lay there wondering how all this would affect our already high river.

Up with the larks again and prepared for every eventuality we put on our wellies ready for the off. Sue's designer welly boots had big daises printed on them - she couldn't wear just ordinary green ones - besides they matched her designer secateurs! We headed for the mill. The river was a muddy brown raging mass of water thundering over the dam and down the waterfalls. Sue was a little apprehensive but I assured her it would not be a problem. After all, the river and mill had been there for hundreds of years.

The next day was bright and sunny again. The river had dropped a bit but was still a dirty brown torrent. Later in the day we went for a walk with Peter and Eileen to visit the Camp de St Judes which is only a few kilometres away but it ended up being a route march. Peter had been there before and was sure he knew the way. Six kilometres later, we reached a memorial site. During the last war it had been a transit camp for Auswitz and other death camps. It also housed thousands of Spanish deportees that were opposing the fascist regime in Spain. At the head of the panoramic view there is a large plaque cast in ceramic and containing photos of the camp as it was. It is now grassed over but it's still a cold reminder of man's inhumanity.

Arriving much later and hungry, back at the campsite we found that we had some new neighbours in their motorhome – a French couple with their dog and cat. The campsite was still empty and very quiet, except for Remy, who was getting everything ready for the start of the season in May.

Our days are filled with visits to the mill, cutting the overgrown bushes, contemplating the project and walks around the area. We are having some lovely sunshine. Sometimes there's a little rain at night but mostly it is warm weather and sometimes quite hot at about 25°. The river is now back to crystal clear but still running fast and everything is growing very quickly.

## Flea market French style

Brocante day at Caussade dawns with a very bright early morning sun. Lovely! It's a nice working town, vibrant at times but with a relaxed air about it. People have time to stop and talk. We hadn't expected anything special, it's a professional Brocante with a couple of car booters thrown in so the prices were high, but it was a change. I noticed a polished butchers' block. I thought - 30 euros that's good - then Sue pointed out it was 830 euros. I wish the French would write clearly, or perhaps I should take more time to read properly. I didn't buy it!

The Brocante is set up around the square. There are flower beds in full bloom, cafés dotted here and there with seating outside, all very civilised. There were some gems amongst the hideous rubbish, mostly fake antiques and one stall looked like someone's barn had been cleared out, judging by the assortment of objects, including rust, dust and any old rubbish that could be sold! We had a wander around the side streets as you always notice something different and I just love old character buildings. A very pleasant morning spent people watching, browsing and discovering. We went for lunch at a café close to the square. The meal was diabolical, we picked over it with our forks and left. We returned to Cayriech. Another café to add to the Gordon Ramsey hit list.

The French couple back at the campsite were sitting out taking in the sun so we walked over to talk to them. Having confidence has never been an issue so I am happy to attempt to talk to anyone of any nationality. It's understanding that has been the biggest hurdle but it is usually overcome a little by the waving of arms and describing, or sky painting. Like I said, I am a demented Englishman! Now I am able to communicate a little better. Between the four of us we talked at length, only in French. It transpired he was just retiring from forty years working as senior Social Security Officer in Montauban. We had a good laugh when I asked when they next come to the village if he could bring his boots and shovel so he could work at our mill - "on the black."

They told us where to buy goods, where to go to see some beautiful and interesting places, even writing down French words for us to remember. There is no doubt speaking French, or trying to speak French, is a must. The young lady at our bank, who is the only one who speaks a little English, said there were so many of the newcomers to the region that don't even try, or want to speak the language. The French strongly resent this.

# Builders head on

I had made a decision to make an early Monday morning start and explore the Bricos (Builders merchants and B & Q type places) getting prices, collecting catalogues and seeing who stocks what. The plan was to drive down to Montauban and work my way back to Cayriech. Well that was the plan! Sue said she wanted to come too.

I had my UK working head on which means I don't hang about. We didn't get off early as planned so we started at the Bricos and builders merchants at Caussade first. Sue shouted, "Slow down," several times as her nails gripped the edge of the seat and, door handle. Her white knuckles showed through! I wasn't used to her new sports car, capable of 130+ mph, it just wants to go quickly! We finally reached Montabaun - after a few arguments. It was mad. We went into the huge Brico Depot. There were trolleys everywhere, people dashing about, staff filling shelves and the checkouts had long queues. "Get me out of here," I screamed in my head.

By now Sue was getting hungry and pretty fed up, because of the numerous "U" turns so we could visit other merchants, things were getting very hectic, cars whizzing about and just missing us we eventually made our way to Albi Sud, another commerce area of Montauban. The air was getting thick in the car so I pulled over and shouted "You drive then." The lunch time closing deadline was fast approaching but we just got to our destination in time to visit one more merchant before they shut down for their long lunch break. My plan was in ruins. Sue was now not talking to me, well just a shout now and again of "Look out." I drove to the autoroute and we got back to Cayriech in record time. Exhausted from the stress and arguments I thought things can only get better!

Tuesday arrives and I decided to let Sue have a complete rest from my manic rushing around and always doing something. I thought I was doing good and making up for yesterday's madness. Not so it was to prove! Just then I found out that Peter had volunteered the pair of us to help Remy move some 3 tonne mobile cabins into place. Half way through the job Peter mentioned that the four of us were going to Cahors that day. No one had bothered to tell me though. But he had arranged it with Sue and Eileen. I was more than a little surprised. Four sweaty hours later we were still at it in the hot sun. Sue was getting pretty mad. Finally, she erupted in a rage and who could blame her. "We were on our holidays," she hollered and stormed off. I got my bike out and went to look for her. I found her by the river and very tearful. It took me all evening and night to smooth things over. I think Peter has lost the plot.

The sun gave way to a showery evening as we waved goodbye to the French couple as they left the campsite. The next day however, the sun was back with a vengeance. It seems to be getting hotter by the day so we had a lazy time. Peter was under strict instructions not to volunteer us for any more work on the campsite. Otherwise Sue and Eileen would bury him in a little plot, and possibly me. Well, I was likely to be found face down in the river. You don't mess around with the fire signs.

We called at our local hardware store, two minutes away in Puylaroque, to pick up our new Stihl chainsaw. My bow-saw was no match for some of the trees we had to cut. Yes, I know I could have bought it cheaper in the UK but we needed it at that moment. I had thought of it before leaving the UK and I could have kicked myself but it is always good to get some things locally. Shopping where you will eventually be living is a goodwill thing.

# Tourists R'us and Peters penance!

Wednesday and it's Eileen's Birthday. The sun was bright and hot and Peter asked if we wanted to go to Cahors with them for the day. I looked up to the skies. It didn't look that promising towards the north. They had been there many times and were a bit stuck in their ways.

After a bit of debate we persuaded them to try somewhere else. During our chats with the French couple about our visit to Rocamadour they had told us about Cordes-sur-Ciel and it wasn't far going via St-Antonin-Noble-Val. "But I am doing the navigating," I said, remembering our little excursion to St Judes Camp!

We set off on our excursion in Peter and Eileen's motorhome. We had planned a leisurely drive. After passing through Septfonds (seven fountains) the next village to us, there is a dead straight Roman road that climbs slowly up above the Aveyron Gorge. The views from the top are fantastic. The road then twists and turns dropping into the gorge finally revealing the medieval town of St Antonin-Noble-Val.

Just before the centre ville, a right turn takes you over the bridge that crosses the wide fast flowing Aveyron river. Then a left turn and through a little tunnel that leads to a lovely valley running alongside the river. A short way further on a red van that had been following us overtook and as it passed the two occupants were waving, tooting the horn and pointing to something. They passed and disappeared off down the road with their hazard lights flashing.

Thinking something was wrong Peter stopped the motorhome. Was one of the cycles hanging off the back? I jumped out and found nothing wrong. We continued our journey. A bit further on we saw the red van in a lay-by and a man standing beside it was flagging us down.

As we slowed to pull in, I put my hand on the nearest heavy thing I could find which happened to be a full litre bottle of vodka. My 90cm heavy crow bar was next to my seat in my own motor home back at Cayriech. Still a bottle would hurt just as well. Was this one of those scams you read about? Perhaps he thought his luck was in as I was wearing a deep pink tee-shirt with white trim and Peter had a dusty pink Fred Perry number on! Sue and Eileen were sitting in the back out of sight chatting, so we might have looked like a couple of effeminate old boys.

The man walked back to us and Peter slid the window open. Before Peter could say a word, the man blurted, "I can see you are English and you obviously don't speak French." We all looked at each other as he continued, "You just came through the tunnel. There is a square plaque that says – "Allumez vos feux" (but in French - it means put your lights on! There have been loads of accidents in there. A motorbike could have run into you and he could have been killed." "Eh!" I exclaimed.

"The police will get you and you will pay a 90 euros fine. You will get caught as the police are watching all the time. I live here! Where are you from?" All said in one breath and the smell of strong stale tobacco wafted in through the open window. His accent and pronunciation of the words of the sign convinced us his French wasn't that good. A few words were exchanged. As he walked back to his van we just sat there open mouthed and dumbstruck. Especially as Peter had put his lights on half way through and the tunnel was lit anyway.

We continued our journey while wondering what on earth that was all about! It was one of those speechless moments. There are some strange people about.

The sun shone brightly as we passed through the valleys and the stunning countryside and arrived in Cordes. We parked a little away from the centre as we didn't know quite what to expect but we had been told by the French couple we met in cayriech, that we would love it.

There was a large site map at the bottom of a narrow cobbled street. It was fairly quiet as we made our way towards the centre ville. There were medieval buildings either side, some were small shops and others were houses. The street steadily got steeper. We passed through a portcullis arch and then a sharp turn and still we were climbing. This must be the centre we thought. But, no! Still we kept climbing, through more arches and more twist and turns. The granite cobbles went on and on. At each turn it seemed to get steeper and revealed more medieval buildings, each one different from the last.

The architecture and the view as I looked back over the higgledy-piggledy roof tops was like looking back into the past. Finally reaching the main street we walked over to a big square. There were restaurants with outside seating on both sides and at the end a long low wall and ledge creating a seat. Looking over the wall the ground disappeared away into an impressive valley. The houses dotted about the wide green expanse looked like little models. The town was obviously geared up for the tourist trade but nonetheless the buildings were beautiful.

Cordes sits high on a hill top, roads and paths are terraced to the top, breathtaking views virtually from all sides of the town, it's obvious that the residents love flowers, there are Planters, large rustic stone troughs and hanging baskets everywhere. The white stone buildings acting as a backdrop for the beautiful lilac wisteria climbing to the rooftops and deep green ivy.

My eyes, constantly aloft looking at the impressive ornate roof overhangs and arched widows, a lot of time is needed to explore this place.

One large gift shop had the most incredible ceiling, built from handmade bricks and an ancient stone sink with taps on one wall. You could just imagine how it must have been in the old days.

After lunch, and a very expensive tiny cup of coffee, we made our way back down. As we neared the bottom it became obvious that we had had a lucky escape. Three coach loads of French tourists had just arrived. As they walked past us ascending to the centre ville we couldn't fail to notice some women wore suits and high heels. They had no idea what lay ahead of them.

If you ever visit take sensible shoes. You will thank me for that advice. Oh and you might need to take some oxygen too!

Our next stop was to be a place called Penne. I deliberately picked a cliff hanging winding forest route for Peter to tackle. A penance for all the trouble he had got me into with Sue.

Winding down through the hairpin bends, Eileen was going green as she peered over the edge, then she covered her eyes. I joked, "Wait until we go on the single track road," but I wasn't joking.

The forest area was lovely and a complete contrast to the green valleys that we had been driving along earlier. There were birds of prey circling in the thermals. There were 100 foot trees towering above us. Then there would be a clearing and a sheer drop revealing a canopy of greens and browns as the trees swirled down into the deep forest valley.

We finally arrived at Penne with Eileen's nerves in tatters. From the parking area we walked down the hill. Most of the French historic towns and villages that we had visited so far seem to have hidden secrets waiting around a corner. Penn was no exception. The main street was like any modern tarmac town road with a couple of medieval buildings thrown in, but once through a small arch, just big enough for a car to pass through, revealed a small church. It was not too obvious where to go. The tiny streets leading to the old houses were only accessible by foot. They had granite cobbles with a central drainage channel. It was so quiet, I could easily imagine what it must have been like in ancient times, with people pulling along hand carts through the narrow streets.

This is a village that time has forgotten. An amazing place with buildings untouched for decades, some still under restoration. There was a finger of land pointing towards the sky, towering high above the village and clearly showing that people once lived on it.

Had this place been in the UK it would have been turned into a theme park with hot dog stalls and children's rides. That's what I like about the places we have seen so far, tourism seems to have been kept to the minimum so that the architecture can be appreciated.

After exploring Penne we left for a leisurely drive back leaving the three coach loads of French tourist to follow our trail. We were so glad we had been one jump ahead of them.

Back in Cayriech we got together for a drink and, of course, the discussion turned to the red van Brit man incident. We laughed our socks off.

# A poke in the eye

The next couple of days were spent cutting and shifting the overgrowth at the mill. In between the showers, the insects came out to play. They were testing their teeth on us. The bites were the size of eggs. Vicious little biters – or words to that effect.

I have always believed things happen for a reason. I stayed behind to do some extra cutting one evening while Sue returned to the motorhome to prepare tea. I found a nice stick for walking and poking stuff with, after finishing the cutting I started wandering back to the campsite with my new walking stick. Remy's mums big brown mean looking dog was on the loose. Previously Peter had assured me it was harmless. The first time I had walked past it, I had crossed to the other side of the lane. As I did not want to make eye contact with it I looked the other way but kept one eye on it to track its whereabouts.

It must have smelt my fear. I had been thinking back to when I was twelve years old. I was doing my paper round at 5.30am along the dark cobblestone backstreets of Bethnal Green and it was pretty creepy. I was chased by a big dog. I only escaped by jumping on car roofs, one to another. The owners never did find out how a row of cars had got dented roofs overnight. But I escaped the dog!

Anyway, back to the big brown dog. The crafty thing crept up behind me with the fur on its back standing on end and showing its teeth. As it came for me I poked it in the eye with my new walking stick. It ran off yelping. When I saw it again, this time it gave me a wide berth and I'm sure it winked at me as I passed. Perhaps it was thinking - wait till you ain't looking then I'll get you back.

Back at the campsite, Sue found it quite amusing, We settled down to watch the TV while having some food. Peter and Eileen's motorhome was parked next to ours. We could see Eileen and their TV through the window, she was engrossed watching her favourite soap, suddenly we heard shouting. Eileen was blaming Peter for changing the TV channels mid programme and switching it off and on. Peter, on the other hand was protesting his innocence, the argument escalated into an almost full blown row.

They settled down when the TV stayed on, suddenly it went off and on again, screams erupted from Eileen. It then dawned on me, every time I pressed the remote for our Hymers heating, it controlled their TV. Oh! What fun and games I played on them after that discovery. Psss! Don't tell them!

# Birthday girl

The sun was out thank goodness despite having had quite a lot of rain overnight and it was Sue's birthday. She opened all her cards brought over from the UK and set them up in the motorhome. Her phone was constantly beeping with text messages from our family. Don't you just love technology!

We planned to go sightseeing and have lunch out somewhere quiet. Remy the campsite owner called by as he had a message for us from the former mayoress. Apparently there was a problem with our Permis de Construire and it needed sorting urgently. We asked if the director of the DDE could help. "No," he said, "the director was director no more. He had taken early retirement." Ooops what's going on? But we can't find out until after the weekend.

There was nothing we could do so we would not let it spoil the day! The car was fuelled up and ready to go off exploring. The sun was getting ever hotter so Sue decided to get her top off! Luverly Juberly!

With the push of a button, in just twenty seconds, the roof folded back and tucked itself into the neat compartment behind the seats of Sue's little sports car. Sue just loves getting her top off! Her little car that is.

All dressed up and ready to go, Sue looked as beautiful as the day we met. We set off for the medieval village of Montricoux to have a little look around en-route to Bruniquel. Hopefully, we can have lunch there.

With the wind in our hair - well what's left of mine - I drove carefully along the tree-lined winding road to Caussade. I didn't want a repeat performance of our excursion to Montauban where we had almost ended up getting divorced following the white knuckle ride I put Sue through!

Driving beneath the canopy of tall plane trees, with the sun's rays flickering through them like strobe lights and with the roof off you have a completely different driving experience. You can hear the birds singing, the breeze in the trees, the smells of the countryside and an undisturbed view skywards. First we see a heron passing like a Concorde with smaller birds diving at it and complaining. Further on a kestrel was hovering just waiting to drop onto its prey. No longer are we cocooned in a tin and glass bubble looking out. We are totally aware of the elements around us. Yes, I was watching the road as well!

From Caussade we took the straight Roman road towards Montricoux. The fields either side were in different states of growth. There were little farms here and there with people busying themselves with their daily chores. It was crisp and clean with the smell of freshly moistened earth after last night's rain. We let the only two cars we saw pass us as we were in no rush.

As we arrived in Montricoux we heard the church bell chime. It was fairly quiet as we walked the short way into the village which had a couple of bars and a few small shops. We found interesting houses and tiny streets. Some of the houses seemed to have been left in the past untouched. The render on the colombage buildings was flaking and the oak timbers showed their age but it all added to the charm and mystery. There were impressive overhangs with their heavy cantilever ornate oak supports. Some of them so close that if you had leaned out of the upstairs window you could have easily reached the opposite house. I just love the designs of medieval buildings.

Getting hungry, we left for Bruniquel, only five minutes away. It was quite a surprise when we got there, a complete contrast, there had been some development. There was a new car-park and restored buildings housing a shop and tourist office. Bruniquel sits on a hill and you can only access it from one side. The other side offers cliff views into a valley and overlooks a river with the road running next to it. The road goes to Penn then onto St Antonin-Noble-Val.

The whole area is steeped in history. There are towns on hills and valleys interconnected by tunnels and rivers. The landscape is stunning and there is plenty of wildlife to be spotted, if you take the time to look.

We parked and made our way up one of the steep streets that leads to the château but before reaching the top, on a little terraced street, we found a Salon de Thé. We had a nice relaxing lunch. It was very clean, the proprietoress was very friendly and we had a chat. All the tarts and cakes were homemade and there was a good selection of teas and freshly ground coffee.

We noticed there were Greek artefacts lying about the shop so we asked about their significance. Apparently she had lived in Greece for some years. We spoke to her in Greek which surprised her! Those two terms of Greek lessons at a Sheffield language school didn't go to waste after all.

Lunch over, we explored the area. We wandered around the gardens and grounds of the Château in the hot sun. The smell of jasmine and the other flowers and herbs brought back memories of our times spent in Cyprus. Even the look and feel of the place was so similar. A beautiful wisteria tree in full bloom, the lilac flowers set against the perfect backdrop of white stone buildings. All very much like Cyprus - until we peered over a stone wall into the lush green valley with the river below.

It was very quiet with just the odd tourist here and there. We met a little party of sightseers over from Canada. We had a chat and one gentleman took our photo for his travel diary. I told him my name, we shook hands, we laughed as we both shared famous writer's names. We wished them well and bon voyage. It's lovely to meet pleasant people.

# Bon voyage to friends

Sightseeing over, we returned to Cayriech. Peter and Eileen were getting ready for their journey back to Lancaster in the morning.

The sun was out and hot but clouds were forming above the surrounding hills.

Taking time out from packing we all attempted to have a game of boule. Well I've tried it. What's all the fuss about? Perhaps I've not slowed down enough yet!

Remy's wife Jocelyne started to walk over in our direction but she stopped and sat on a low wall in a flood of tears. We went over to comfort her. It would have been her son's 22nd birthday the following day, it was one of those moments. She was inconsolable for a time. We had learned the full tragic circumstances leading up to his death last September first hand, thankfully dispelling hearsay that we did not believe one bit. He was a lovely young man and our memories of him were of him chatting and playing with the girls in the pool and always being very polite. Jocelyne just had to talk to someone as Remy threw himself into work and their daughter Marianne went away for a few days. Each were dealing with the painful time in their own way.

We had planned on going out to dinner with Alan and Viv for Sue's birthday. They are completing a new build north of us and Peter and Eileen were getting an early night before departing for the UK.

Our friends picked us up as we can't fit four in the sports car. Arriving in Caussade we ended up at a pizza house. I am coeliac which is a bit of a strange place to eat! Our friends had eaten there before and said they have a selection of other dishes. To cut a long story short, I told the owner the meal was diabolical and he had the cheek to knock off just one drink from the bill. Yet another restaurant on the Gordon Ramsey hit list. It was basic cooking, nothing fancy, but how can so many people get it wrong? Sue's evening had gone down the pan, but Alan and Viv's company made up for the terrible meal!

Sunday morning we had a good laugh about the disastrous meal and vowed never again to eat out. Peter and Eileen said we should have stayed and had a meal with them!

After breakfast we waved goodbye to Peter and a tearful Eileen. They had a fourteen hundred kilometre drive ahead of them before reaching Lancaster.

The campsite was empty apart from one resident Frenchman, Jacques, who lives in a caravan for six months in Cayriech. He then flies to Moscow for the rest of the year. If the cold war was still active I would be sure he was a spy!

# Wild rivers flow

The Tranquillity of the afternoon in the hot sun made us feel very relaxed. We decided to have a leisurely wander around the park and village. We hadn't got that far when we noticed dark clouds forming on the surrounding hills, we could feel the rain was on its way, so we returned to our motorhome.

After our meal – disaster. It could not have been worse. The expected rain came. And came it did! For the next 3 days and nights we had heavy rain. I popped down to the mill in the breaks to see how high the river was rising.

It was a dirty, brown, thundering mass of water. So much so, that the waterfalls had disappeared beneath the deep water. Sue was concerned. I, on the other hand, was pleased to see it in this state. I now knew that where it had breached the bank a little in places, I could make repairs and diversions for future flood protection.

After a couple of days of this Sue was getting despondent. The weather was grim and she was getting motorhome fever. Luckily we had satellite TV. I told her it wouldn't last, but being cooped up together in a small space was no fun. Good job we weren't in a tent!

The rain eased so we decided to visit an acquaintance that I had met in the UK and who lived about half an hour away. They were a very nice family with two young sons and they had spent the last five years renovating their house - and still ongoing. Later that evening the weather changed again. The sky cleared and stars were shining bright. We were in for a cold night.

# Let the sun shine bright

The next morning it was hazy but the sun was trying to emerge. It was only a matter of time. Then like throwing a light switch on the sun burst through and burnt off the remaining moisture. We were so pleased and relieved. To make the most of it we hurriedly went to the mill to do some work until it got too hot.

The next couple of hot sunny days were spent clearing the area around the mill by thinning the overgrowth. It was during this time we made a couple of discoveries. Unbeknown to us, the previous owner had put in an underground telecom line from the village to our gate, what a bonus!

Taking a rest in the shade we noticed a lizard sitting on a log, it seemed to be waving every so often with its front right foot. Then we noticed another lizard on a rock close by waving back in the same way. Very strange we thought. Then we remembered the Planet Earth programme on amphibians and reptiles where there was one species of frog close to extinction that waved in the same way. It was signalling to its neighbour to stay away as this is my territory. So have we made a startling discovery? I now have to try and film its little act!

In SW France temperatures can reach minus 15 deg & below.
Hymer wrapped up with thermal screens in minus 6 degrees.

Cayriech, Camping Le Clos de la Le're

# In Search of the Source!

Our days are spent doing a little work on the land, walking the country lanes that follow the river and talking to everyone we met. The river is now back to its old self and flows with crystal clear spring-like water. Sparkling in the bright sun, the spray from the waterfalls causes the occasional little rainbow. Fish are plentiful and there's two visiting ducks.

We went back to the campsite and spoke to Remy about how clear the river was. "Ah"! he said, "it's the source." He explained, in French, that there was an underground geyser that is known locally as the source. He went on to explain how to find it. Well we think we knew what he said. Anyway, we decided to pop along in the car to have a look to see where our river Le're starts its journey.

We arrived at mill number one on the river Le're, an Auberge . We put on our walking boots and followed the river. Are we trespassing? We thought, but we don't know for sure, Remy told us it was this way, at least I think I understood his instructions.

We continue on through the deep undergrowth following an obviously little used track. There were twists and turns and waterfall after waterfall. We finally emerge, after fighting our way out of very dense undergrowth and a little wood. It was amazing. No not the source but a hidden valley.

The valley was an elongated half circle. On the curved side was a steep tree-lined limestone hill and at one end it turned into a limestone cliff. On our left-hand side was the river. Then, there was dense forest with a similar hill behind it. The whole area was about ½ km long and was completely enclosed by the terrain. This flat basin was covered with lush green planting. There was nothing around except for wildlife noises. We continued on our search. It was getting hotter by the minute. Approaching the end of the valley where it closed up to create a narrow gorge, there was a 100 foot high rock face to our right and a steep dense forest to our left. We could hear the river below – somewhere. We approached a small gap. Here the temperature had changed from hot to cool in this dark sheltered area. There were large rocks lying about that had obviously fallen down from the rock-face high above. We cautiously hurried through.

The track now narrowed but we were out into the sunlight again. We walked further on but still no sign of the source. It was getting hotter and we weren't fully prepared for what seemed to be an endless trail. After about three kilometres we decided to turn back.

Once we were back at the campsite we questioned Remy. We even drew a picture of where we had walked. Yes, we were on the right trail but it was further on, we'll know in the future! We relaxed for the rest of the day and the next one in the hot sun.

# Birthday boy

It was our friend Alan's birthday and we were invited to dinner in their mobile home. Their house is not finished yet. They had arranged a little excursion for us to Mont-St-Cyr which was to the north of them, we didn't know what to expect but it was well worth the journey.

We arrived at a viewing point high above Cahors. The impressive panoramic view of Cahors below was fantastic. You could see for miles. The river Lot was winding around below and the boats looked like little toys. It gave a fantastic view of the whole area showing the old and new town. It was quite odd seeing cars and people in miniature moving around, there was no noise everything was so far away, just birds chirping and a slight breeze where we stood gazing. What a sight!

We finished the day with a mouth watering evening meal cooked by Viv. Great conversation was had by all, although, Alan and I went on a bit too much about building, so we were told by Sue and Viv. We didn't know what all the fuss was about we were on a building site after all!

Friends and new acquaintances gathered for sad goodbyes to
the UK.  Remy, Left , Jocelyne fourth from left

Comical noisy neighbours in Cayriech

## Searching the source continues

A lazy Sunday start as it was hot again. Far too hot to work on the land so we got ready for another search for La Source! Backpack, water, food and camera with us this time. We arrived at the first mill again and made our way to the track. But before we had got very far we were stopped by a man who told us we were trespassing. He asked us to leave but suggested that we could drive further up the road and take another track.

We found the new route and it took us into the valley. Once again we were in awe of the surroundings that were magical. There were wild flowers, tiny powder blue butterflies drinking in the small pools of water left over from the downpour and strange bird sounds, almost like monkeys calling. We went through the gorge even quicker this time walking the winding track. The river disappeared from sight and sound at times so we had to stop and listen to make sure we were going the right way. We followed the sound of the river cascading over the many waterfalls in the distance.

We had walked for two hours, finding more hidden valleys and more wildlife, even the sound of an eagle calling high above us but still no sign of the illusive source. We came across a road. We could hardly believe our eyes. All this walking when we could have got to this point by driving. By this time Sue was getting tired so we stopped and had some lunch.

I decided to see if the road would be quicker than walking back along the track to our parked car. I left Sue to rest and I walked up the long hill. I saw a church in the distance but nothing much else. The whole area was deserted. I realised the road was going in the wrong direction so I returned back to where Sue was waiting. I had been gone for 20 minutes it was a hard climb on the hot tarmac.

The Impressive stonework built into the rock face at Rocamadour

# Lynx but not deodorant

There was nothing for it but to give up our search for the source and go back the way we had come. Occasionally Sue would stop walking and start listening, thinking she could hear something in the undergrowth moving about. We looked around but the forest was too dense.

We stopped next to the river to eat a lovely juicy melon. Thank goodness, that melon was packed in my rucksack and had been digging in my back for the whole journey. Washing in the crystal clear river we noticed there were a couple of ancient ruined houses nearby. How odd as they were miles from anywhere.

On the way back we came to a ford. Sue heard noises again in the surrounding wood, we had to make a detour off the path and through the wood as the ford was too deep and wide to cross. I noticed the water had just been disturbed so I investigated. There was a very big paw print from a large cat and another elongated smudged one. I assumed it was made by the big animal retreating from the water in haste. We scanned the surrounding area with excitement.

Walking further back on the track we found another paw print next to a muddy puddle. I decided to photograph it. When we got back to the campsite we asked Remy about the infamous source. He assured us it was just further on. When we asked how much farther, he couldn't remember!

We told him about the paw print, and he knew exactly what it was. "Le grand lynx," he said. It had been spotted in the woods...Wow!

The search for the source is to continue. Let's hope the lynx is more afraid of us if our paths should cross again!

The dramatic Rocamadour! An outstanding achievement by builders over the decades protecting this magical town from decay

# Oh! Not another search for the source!

A couple of lazy days. Where do the mornings go? We seemed to be in a time warp - well, at least two hours behind. We had travelled over to France when the clocks changed and two hours had just vanished.

A very wet Monday morning. Ugh! We awoke to hear heavy rain pounding on the motorhome roof. Dark clouds everywhere. Could it be a repeat of last week when we were stuck inside the motor home. "How long will it last," Sue asked, looking fed up. After lunch there was a break in the downpour so we grabbed our wet weather gear and walking boots. The search for the source was on again.

I checked the map and found the road I had discovered on our previous quest. By driving there we were able to knock 4 kilometres off of trekking through the woods and valleys. We parked up and found another small overgrown track following the river Le're. This route was obviously older than the other ways we had tried previously. The gorge was getting narrower and steeper either side and Remy had told us it was further on.

We entered a very old damp forest that resembled the swamps of the deep south of the USA. There were very old trees all draped in moss. It was dark and eerie with a strange stillness all around. But it wasn't long before we could hear the gentle trickling sound of the narrow but fast flowing river. The odd bird called here and there. Then, ancient walls and ruins. The name on the bridge where the track started "Le Le're Mort" was quite apt. We had to pass under barbed wire stretched across the path so it seemed that we were trespassing but who would see us in this wet wilderness! Besides, it was non-working day, Le Lundi.

The forest sides closed in on us with the river narrowing but still crystal clear. We had to climb the steep hill occasionally to avoid the river as it had overflowed in places. The path now disappeared under thick undergrowth and loose rocks, tree roots and fallen trees covered in moss made our progress very slow. We anticipated meeting some strange toothless hillbilly carrying a gun at any moment, I started to sing the tune of the dueling banjos from the film Deliverance, "shut up! You're giving me the creeps" Sue said. How much farther is the source?

Not wanting to be defeated we carried on. We were getting very close to the Caylus army training camp area, as we suddenly heard loud automatic gun fire. Had we wandered into the training zone? We looked at each other and decided to make a hasty retreat. If a mad gun toting man or a hungry lynx didn't get us then perhaps a stray bullet would! Will we ever find the source?

We took a different route back to Cayriech that ended up being tiny single track roads in the middle of nowhere, high above the woods where we had just been. We happened upon a couple of very strange men walking along in the rain. One was very tall and thin and carrying an axe. The other one was shorter and fatter. They both had a wild look about them and both were dressed very oddly for the weather. They were soaked through and filthy dirty. We were so glad we hadn't met them in the woods. Pooh and pants came to mind!

Just a glimpse of the impressive and intricate column design at the Place Royale Montauban

Exploring the delights of Cordes sur Ciel

One of the many portcullis entrances at Cordes sur Ciel

# French networking

Back at the campsite, the rain eased and we chatted to our French neighbours who were on holiday for two weeks. They were the same age as us and très agréable the language barrier came into play but we had fun trying and added a few new words to our vocabulaire!

"Il fait beau aujourd'hui" Remy called as we passed by for a early morning trip to Caussade to do some shopping.

Later we went for lunch at the Vieux de Moulin, an Auberge situated next to the River Le're but quite hidden, it seemed to be popular with the locals and they streamed in as the clock struck twelve. We thought we were out of luck as the seats started filling, but the waiter beckoned us in.

He spoke little English so I passed him my diet card written in French telling him about my allergy and what I couldn't eat "Pas de problème Monsieur" he replied.

He disappeared into the kitchen, a few moments later the door opened, with smiling faces the chef and waiter told us they had enough food, thank goodness. We were told by Jocelyne, Remy's wife the food was très bon et pas cher!

It was very French, a large old mill house. We could have been in someone's cosy front room. Sitting at the tables were a wide selection of people and one by one they greeted us with a cheery Bonjour.

We sat down next to an elderly lady who spoke a little English. So we got talking and it wasn't long before she had invited us to visit her home. A well dressed chap, also on our long table, decided he could speak a little English and, after a lengthy conversation, it turned out he owned a large chunk of Puylaroque, the nearest village. He was also a research and design director of an international development company in the building industry, he too asked us to visit him at his house to give him some advice on secondhand excavators and where he could buy them in the UK. At the end of the 2 hour lunch, the longest time we had spent having lunch in France so far, we had met several nice people and expanded our list of interesting contacts.

You wont find big 4X4's in the tiny streets of Penne

# Fairy tale castles

May Day was here. In the early hours I could hear cars dashing passed the campsite which was very unusual. I lay in bed wondering where everyone was going. The coast maybe? Visiting far off relatives, that's the usual May Day thing. I drifted back off to sleep.

Crikey, now I've overslept! Not like me. A very lazy start. Is the Brico open? I needed some bolts to fix my new box to the trailer. After breakfast and a visit several minutes away in Caussade it was obvious this is not the UK. Here in this little bit of France they take holidays seriously the Brico was closed. It was now 10.30 and we were on our way back to Cayriech. I turned to Sue. "What do you reckon, Carcassonne?" "Yes, why not," she replied.

Back at the motorhome we hastily packed food and drink into our picnic backpack. " Have we got everything?" I ask Sue. "Yes" she replied, I locked the motorhome door, put everything into the boot of the car, just about to drive off, Oh! I've forgotten my sunglasses I say, "can we never just set off in one go" Sue says. It's an age thing!

We finally set off to Caussade for some fuel. The roads were quiet. We soon picked up the southbound autoroute. It's was the first time we had been further south than Montauban. It's another little adventure.

Carcassonne is just over a couple of hours away from our little bit of France. We had read about it on the internet and got a lot of information from one of the French forums and members.

It was a very sunny hot day so we had the roof down for a leisurely drive. Well it started out like that but I put my foot down once on the autoroute. After some very stern words from Sue I slowed down.

We took in the sights and the landscape. Driving past industrial areas beside the autoroute gave me a chance to add companies of interest to my memory bank. A Big Mat a few minutes south of Montauban, fantastic, just what we will need for our re-build. We soon reached Toulouse and passed the aerospace centre on our right. "We will have to explore that one day," Sue said. There's so much to see I don't know how we will find the time!

After Toulouse the autoroute climbs away. At the top we get our very first clear glimpse of the snow capped Pyrénées. We were like a couple of kids asking, "Can we see the sea yet Dad?" The best things in life never change. The road drops away into a vast wide breathtaking valley and you can see for miles.

We noticed an Aire stopover next to the Canal du Midi so we pulled off the autoroute. It was busy with families with their huge cool boxes all sitting at wooden tables or on the grass. The French, as always, were taking their leisure seriously. They were eating and relaxing, taking time, walking their dogs and playing with the children.

We found a spot next to the canal and had a relaxing late lunch whilst watching cyclists passing on the towpath. We imagined the time when Rick Stein passed through here on a barge cooking lovely regional dishes as he went along. After lunch we walked a short way to one of the lock gates. The canal level changes about twenty feet. What a lovely place and it's all free!

The traffic was very light for a Mayday compared to the UK. We would not even have contemplated venturing out on a bank holiday. A visit to the coast from Barnsley, almost half the distance we were travelling today, would have meant up to three hours in traffic jams each way.

We made good progress southbound with the sun beating down upon us. Suddenly, a huge lizard, it's body held high off the tarmac and with it's legs stretched to the limit raced across the autoroute just in front of us, Its legs were going like the clappers, an amazing comical sight. I hope it got across all six lanes safely.

Finally reaching Carcassonne with the sun high, bright and hot but thankfully there was a cooling breeze. We stopped off at the old bastide quarter first. The matrix design of the streets, crisscrossing each other with tall buildings either side and huge high window shutters meant the sunlight was blocked out for a good part of the day.

We found the big square, the centre piece so common with this type of architecture. It was the usual sight of tables set out in the middle, little cafés on the perimeter and people sitting, eating, drinking and chatting. Numerous pigeons were flying around looking for titbits. All very relaxing in this mini city.

Just a handful of shops were open. We passed one small shop that was being fitted out. The obvious owners were looking anxious and giving out instructions to the workers who were outside painting the frontage. Oh how I felt for them having been in this situation many times in the last 30 years. Sue would say, "Why are you doing it? They wont erect a monument to you!" She was right of course. While normal fathers were with their kids I would be working but that's how the industry was. We had to work when the shops were closed

After a short wander we returned to the car and drove to La Cité Médiéval. We parked at the bottom car park close to the river and made our way up. It was quite apparent that this was a bank holiday and probably not the best day to have had a good look around.

As we got towards the top of the hill we came to a motorhome parking area which seemed to be completely full. There were motorhomes parked in the central area and obviously they were settled in for the night. There were others jockeying and circling around looking for a place. Like Indians attacking the wagon train, if one left then another raced to get the vacant space. You could see the gritted teeth of the drivers as they missed their chance. It was turning into a fun people watching day!

We arrived at the drawbridge gate and all I could think of was the Knights of the Round Table. There was even a moat - dried up of course. This was the very first time I had ever seen a building like this before, except as a boy watching TV and films.

There were high round turrets with pointed roofs and vertical slots in the walls for long bows. Oh, I don't count the Tower of London which was my favourite haunt as a nipper as that was local!

By the drawbridge there was a colourful old merry-go-round full of kids and adults. We splashed out on the calèche (horse drawn cart) tour of the ramparts. We joined the rest of the passengers and listened to the drivers commentary, in French of course. I could pick out the odd word, which was mostly travaux and rampart, and I laughed when everyone else laughed. It was fun and it was hot but there was a strong chilly wind in places.

The walk in the inner cité was a little difficult at times as the streets were packed shoulder to shoulder. Buskers were playing on several corners and there was a fun band to keep everyone entertained. The beautiful medieval buildings and the magnificent ornate stonework on the church were very impressive. As was the hotel where we had a coffee in a little salon de thé just to get away from the crowds and have a rest.

After a good look around we decided to battle our way through even more hoards of people still arriving. Zig-zaging down the narrow winding streets we finally made it to the drawbridge and back to the car. Walking over to the river and bridge was tricky as cars dashed in all directions and made crossing the road very hazardous.

We headed back up the autoroute. By now it was getting late but the sun was still hot. We took our time as it gave us a chance to look at the countryside. We saw little church spires with clusters of red tiled shallow pitched roofs dotted about them. There was so much to discover in this wonderful country.

Arriving back at the campsite we were greeted by our French neighbours. They are so nice and friendly and we had a good chat about our adventures that day. They had been to Cordes and swapping notes and going over the maps with them was fun.

Our French was very slightly expanding, Sue had immersed herself in a variety of French books, I on the other hand listened to French CD's, reading is not my strong point! But nonetheless it helped us to converse a little more with a very enthusiastic husband and wife from Northern France.

# New Mayor

The next morning I went to do the washing up that had been left from the day before at the campsite facilities. There were some new arrivals so I said bonjour. I suppose I was getting quite convincingly French, as the man said bonjour back. It was apparent he was not French. He then started to talk to me in English with a French accent. Then he realised I was English and slowly his accent changed to Brummie. (Birmingham) I had trouble keeping a straight face. I covered it up by getting fairy liquid bubbles up my nose and I started sneezing. Then I went into a laughing fit. I chucked the dishes and plates into my basket and made a quick exit back to the motorhome. Telling Sue she choked on her grapefruit laughing!

The rest of the day we relaxed and later visited our neighbour the farmer Monsieur Rivie're and his family for the afternoon. His children were learning English at school and they liked to practice with us. We talked about his dairy herd and milk prices, comparing them with the English price per litre and the different breeds. I was glad I had taken an interest in our local farm in Barnsley where I have 120 metres of Victorian stone stored for the extension of our building. Farming has always been an interest of mine, I suppose it's a nature thing and a dream of getting self sufficient. A delightful afternoon was had under the shade of a large tree in the garden just drinking and talking.

Tomorrow was to be our last day before our departure back to the UK.

We planned an early start as it was going to be a very hot day, the forecast was for 29°. So I am up before the larks. I started to dismantle the safari room that was attached to our motorhome awning. There was so much stuff to shift. Building stuff, cutting kit as well as all the camping gear. We had to drive to Caussade to fill up with diesel as the day after would be Sunday. I should have topped up when we arrived as the price had risen over the last weeks!

After shopping at the Intermache and getting stocked up with food for our return journey we arrived back at the campsite and there was a message waiting for us. We were invited to the new Mayor's inauguration soiree. A short walk to the deserted village had us wondering had we got the message wrong? Hearing voices echoing through the arch next to the church, we walked through and found everyone from the village mingling with drinks and getting to know each other in the little square behind the church. We got a warm welcome from everyone. I got several top ups from a duck shaped orange fountain. I am not a big drinker and after 4 large glasses I felt a bit squiffy. I didn't know it was punch! It seemed to improve my French though.

The party then moved into the community hall, a large restored medieval building. There were long tables covered with crisp white table cloths, hand crafted place names and sprigs of fresh floral and fauna from the surrounding area. A beautiful setting for the 200 or so villagers and the food and wine flowed. We were introduced to the only other British couple that lived in Cayriech. Everyone was so friendly including the new Mayor, Monsieur Jean-Louis Donnadieu who lived locally.

Sue asked if the main meal contained flour. Unfortunately it did! Without delay the waitress scurried off to inform the Mayor who quickly sent over an abundance of fresh salad and charcuterie together with a large glass of vin blanc. This is my kind of Mayor.

Some hours later after speeches and overconsumption of well, just about everything, we followed the villagers out into the sunshine and said our goodbyes. What a wonderful afternoon.

# Lost in translation

I had left the rest of the packing until after the party as it was just too hot. We weren't looking forward to returning to the doom and gloom of the UK anyway.

A new French family arrived at the campsite and the chap made a point of telling me he was a Jehovah's Witness and was here for the conference tomorrow. "Oh!" I said and thought nothing more of it. He wished us well for our journey home. It was getting dark so I finished packing what I could and left the rest for the next day.

Another bright morning and I couldn't sleep. It was a very peaceful normal Sunday morning. I got dressed in my old clothes and then, suddenly at 7.30, the silence was broken as a PA system fired up announcing something I couldn't understand followed by music. Amy Winehouse echoed around the village. "What's going on?" hollered Sue. I told her about my conversation with the Jehovah's Witnesses. Oh my god! Is the new mayor one of them? Is the conference in the village hall? Are we going to be overrun with people calling at our door from now until doomsday? I will have to build a moat and fit electric gates.

I left Sue to try and get back to sleep and trotted off down to our mill. What a relief. I discovered there was a cycle race starting from the village. The penny had finally dropped. The previous Friday we had had a chance meeting with our new mayor when he was helping to prepare the hall. We were out having a walk with our French camping neighbours. They all got talking, the words went into one long fast French conversation, totally incomprehensible except for the odd word like, "vélo." So that's what it was all about! I breathed a sigh of relief.

I arrived at the mill and what a wonderful morning it was. The river was settled and so crystal clear I could see beaucoup de poissons. There were numerous birds singing away. I walked carefully so that I could get a glimpse of any wildlife before my approach disturbed them. I was hoping that I could spot the red squirrel seen previously. Sue's eagle eye saw it one day when we had a visitor to the mill. Bob was a lone traveller from the States. We had invited him into our motorhome one evening and we had a lovely chat. Since his wife had died many years ago he had been on many adventures including sailing the Pacific single handed in a thirteen metre cutter. He had started out from Seattle and got as far as Panama but tiredness and age got the better of him.

He had left the States disillusioned. He felt the country was ruled by money and greed. He was a very polite and gentle person. I should think he was in his early seventies but very slim and fit. He was travelling around in a camper hoping to find a nice little spot of France to call home. He had been living in France for four years and was still trying to get into the French health system. We do hope things turn out well for him and our paths cross again!

Clearing up the trees we had felled several days beforehand took over an hour. I left the last two 4 metre straight trunks till last. It was getting very hot and I was tiring. It took every ounce of energy to drag them from the top field to the grange. Sometimes only a metre at a time before a count of un, deux, trois, Allez! Finally they were under cover so they can dry out. They should be useful for the rebuild.

I walked back to the campsite. The race was in full swing. Cheerful bonjours all round as I passed. I told Sue of my findings. She laughed and said, "You and your scenarios." Oh well, lost in translation again.

# The long goodbye

The lengthy process of packing everything and loading the car on the trailer is like a jigsaw. Things have to fit a certain way or they don't fit at all. On the other hand, Sue just dumps stuff in the cupboards and shuts them quick to stop the contents from escaping.

For the last six weeks I have been sharing the undies cupboard with Sue. I lift the door, reach in and, nine times out of ten, I have a nylon pop sock stuck to my rough hands or I lasso a bra when reaching for my boxers. Or, even worse, a thong mysteriously finds its way down the leg of my boxers and I put them on only to find I have a thong hanging out like a large piece of dental floss!

Our French neighbours called by to say bon voyage et bon courage! We took photos and exchanged email address. They were going to the Sunday market in St Antonin.

I beavered away getting the motorhome ready for the long journey. Just strapping the car down takes a lot of time. By now it was 11.30am and we were ready to leave. I suddenly realised I had been talking to myself in French whilst loading everything. I had a giggle to myself and thought I must have been going mad.

Remy and Jocelyne came to see us off. Just then our friends arrived back from the market. They were surprised but pleased to see we were still there. After yet more photos and kisses on both cheeks we drove out of the campsite. As we passed through the village we saw that the cycle race was at an end. The cyclists were sat at long tables having a barbecue. They gave us cheerful waves and we were off!

Architectural delights of Penne

# Taking our time

It was a beautiful day. We purposely drove through Caussade to have one last look rather than go the long way round the little ring road. There were quite a few people about sitting outside the cafés. "Wish we could stay," I said to Sue. Through the péage we head north on the new autoroute. So much has happened since passing this way southbound almost six weeks earlier.

We decided to stop at an Aire north of Cahors for some late lunch. Our plan was to get as far north of Limoges as possible for our overnight stopover. Come 7pm the sun was still bright and we find a quiet Aire. I set up the satellite dish so Sue can watch the TV then got out our table and chairs and put them outside the motorhome. I positioned them so I could sit and watch the setting sun as I was typing away on the laptop catching up with stories. Taking advantage of a cool breeze while watching the wildlife was very relaxing

A pleasant and undisturbed night's sleep was had, even for a autoroute Aire. While eating breakfast we watched the colourful birds feeding on seeds in the grass from our motorhome window. Again it was a very sunny morning. Our rest over we continued our journey north.

It was smooth going and we reached the north of Orleans by lunchtime. Wherever we stop people come to talk to us. It is so lovely. A French couple on a motorbike from Paris were returning home from touring the South West Coast and two chaps from the UK who were down delivering a load of British timber for their house in France and were taking their hire lorry back to the UK.

We had made a lot of time up and we didn't want to spend a whole night and day in Calais so I decided to take a different route via Rouen. What a big mistake. The last time we went this way it was Winter and on a Sunday. Today, however, the traffic was bad. Heavy lorries trundling towards us on the narrow roads at speed, sometimes too close for comfort. Sue hated it and she hated it even more when we hit the numerous roundabouts and traffic. I had had enough. I cut across country and made for a stopover at Les Andeleys which is east of Louviers with a fairly big campsite next to the Seine. The charges for one night seemed expensive compared to other campsites but we stayed anyway.

After tea we decided to go for a walk but we didn't get far. We got talking to a small group of pensioners on a cycling and camping holiday. They were a jolly lot and we all had a good laugh and chin wag on many subjects. We had just got enough time to walk across the bridge over the Seine, watching the many huge barges passing some with cars on the back of them. The sun slowly dropped out of the sky and it was a beautiful night.

The ruined castle high up on the hill above Les Andelys was lit up and looked très interessant. If we get time it would be nice to visit tomorrow.

The morning was rather chilly with a heavy dew, but, we were next to the river. Breakfast over we packed up and were ready to leave by 12pm. We thought we would have a walk into the old town and were just about to set off when a man stopped to say hello. We got talking. Well talk about a small world. They were from Barnsley and they lived just five minutes from Sue's shop. They were off visiting friends near La Rochelle and Pons. After a lot of talking and goodbyes to the pensioner cycling team we were too late for sightseeing.

We set off for Calais across country to avoid Rouen. We arrived with four hours to spare. We made our way to the motorhome parking area next to the sea and planned to have a look around. It was obvious there were a lot of Brits about as every second car had Brit plates. No sooner had we parked up than someone tapped on our window. "Are you Steve and Sue?" he asked. We were taken aback. Apparently he had had a text message from our friends Peter and Eileen from Lancaster to keep a look out for us. What a chance meeting! This was the first time we had stopped at the parking area and then only found it by chance. The retired couple from Preston were on their way home from wintering in Spain. They were a day early for the ferry crossing.

Time flew by but we had to leave for the tunnel. It would be the first time we had travelled by Eurotunnel. Prior to this it was always too expensive, but after a bit of advice from a fellow traveller we had managed to get a cheap ticket. It worked out just a little more expensive than the ferry.

We arrived at check in an hour early and punched in our number. It asked if we wanted to leave early at no extra charge so I pressed yes! It was as simple as that. We squeezed onto the train. The trailer had just six inches clearance either side. What a truly pleasant journey and we didn't have to leave the comfort of our motorhome.

It was great to avoid the long crawl up the hills out of Dover. As we drove out of the terminal the sun was a huge deep red ball in the sky. We were so glad we had missed the rain a couple of days earlier. My plan was to get clear of the M25 and head north on the old A1, Great North Road. The M1 was always too busy and stopping to sleep on the services is far too noisy and some are limited to only 2 hours stopping time. We were certainly spoilt in France for stopping places.

I had to drive until quite late. Sue was asleep in the comfy Hymer recliner seat next to me. All the parking areas were full with lorries and it wasn't until I got north of Peterborough that I found a quiet place away from the road to park for the night. I jumped into bed and went into a coma until six thirty the next morning.

After breakfast the rest of the journey was uneventful. We arrived at the flat by 8.30. It was very strange as our two Siamese cats stopped in their tracks, gave us very wary looks until we spoke to them reassuringly. They then came up to us to have a good smell. We gave them a good cuddle and they soon settled down. We were back but we were not at home!

# Home! But not with heart

The shop was now open and we had customers calling in to see Sue. The jungle drums were beating. My phone rang. "Are you back yet?" "Can you dig a trench and lay 1000 metres of pipe for us?" Nothing changes!

We ran the gauntlet of ASDA shopping. Pushing, shoving, bad tempers, impatient people and nowhere to park. It was horrendous. Beam us back to Cayriech Scottie!

It was lovely to see our family. The only nice thing about being back.

Friday evening was very warm and people were outside drinking till late at the pub across the road from our flat. Later on there was screaming and shouting. It was Nutter's R Us night. Please beam us up Scottie. The next morning the new bus shelter's glass was in a shattered heap on the floor. Yep! We were back in Barnsley!

# The bigger plan

It was no surprise that during our last visit to Cayriech we came to the obvious conclusion that any serious work that was to be done on the mill would need some serious equipment. We could hire it locally and get everything delivered but the dilemma was that we already had all the building equipment required in Barnsley. We had to weigh up the pros and cons of getting our truck, digger and everything needed for a long stay over there, plus the very long journey down.

The convenience of collecting materials with our own tipper and not having to worry about a hired digger sitting idle at great expense would relieve any pressure on us. We didn't want pressure as we have a lot of that in the UK. Our eventual move to France was supposed to dispense with all of life's pressures. Well that was the thinking!

So planning our digging trip to France seemed simple. We just get loaded up, drive to Dover, board the ferry to France and drive down to the south. Hey presto!

It couldn't be further from the truth.

Relaxing after some hard work at the Moulin. Camping Le Clos de la Le're.
The thermal screen, trying to keep out the relentless 97 degrees heat Phew!

# Don't forget the tent!

Sorting out cat sitters, staff cover for Sue's shop and deliveries was just the tip of the iceberg. At times there seemed to be a conspiracy to keep us in the UK.

Our new operator's licence for the truck didn't come through until the last minute. Even careful planning and deciding to load most of the kit the day before departure, so we could get an early start, simply went out of the window.

Sue woke me at 4am as she couldn't sleep which means neither could I. Reluctantly I got up. We must have had only a few hours in bed and there was still plenty to do.

Stress kicked in at about 8am. I am still loading up the truck with everything, including a portaloo. I was supposed to be taking the heavy duty scaffolding to France but the clock was ticking, I looked at it stacked in the workshop, there just wasn't enough time to load it all, "Sod it." I said to myself, the aluminium tower that was already on the truck would just have to do.

10am arrived and I was still loading when Rhona, who works for Sue, arrived to open Sue's shop and is surprised to see us. She had a good laugh anyway, saying, "I knew you would still be here."

I was wandering about like a headless chicken transferring camping gear from the motorhome to the truck but I left the tent stacked to one side and told myself not to forget to load it.

Our CAT excavator and trailer were stored at a farm a few minutes away and when I collected it I noticed a couple of lights were out. "Bugger!" Yet another job to do! When I got back to the flat I went to look in the stores for light bulbs. "Bugger!" again. No double filament 24volt lamps and you can't just buy them anywhere!

By now it was 11.30. Suddenly a truck pulled up in front of our shop. It was a big delivery of Christmas stock and it had arrived several weeks early. Sue had no choice but to unpack and check everything off with Rhona. Customers arriving at the tea room called out a familiar phrase, "Are you still here? Thought you would have been halfway to France by now."

Stress levels were reaching braking point. Sue followed me up to our flat above the shop. "You've left everything to the last minute," she screamed out. Our two Siamese cats flew out of the room. Well to be exact they skidded, running on the spot on the polished oak floor like a couple of cartoon cats. Eventually they got some traction and ran and hid under the bed!

I shouted back, "I haven't had a minute in the last few months to leave it to the last minute. I aint got enough minutes in a second! There was a blank expression on Sue's face but I knew what I meant. I stormed outside clutching more stuff to load on the truck.

A little later, and calmer, the trailers lights were fixed and some spares stored. At last everything was packed in the large walk-in workshop body of the truck. The cooler was plugged in. Fresh salad and food for the journey, kettle, power inverter, Yorkshire tea bags - must not forget them - anything and everything for a comfortable stay in a tent was loaded. Well it was a first for me and Sue. In 35 years we had never spent the night in a tent! Sue was apprehensive to say the least.

We finally said our goodbyes to Rhona and our two sons who had arrived to see us off. Sue gave our two cats a final cuddle. We popped into the shop to say bye to our regular customers. Just one last check before we set off...Bugger! The tent!...I think I had better load it. Sue gave me something of a sideways glance.

# Heading south at last

Thank goodness, we were off at last - 1.30 pm and only 5 ½ hours late! What a marathon.

We joined the M1 and headed for the Great North Road (A1). I switched on the truck's computer, clicked on the cruise control and put my feet up as we headed south for Dover. As usual I started asking, "Sue have you got the passports, etc., etc?" Yet another sideways glance, I decided to shut up.

We text a French forum member to say that we were on our way down for a rendezvous on the motorway. We had to pick up a digger bucket that was destined for France. On the way we stopped at a Marks & Spencer motorway services for a coffee and bought some boxes of chocolates and biscuits. Our French friends just love them.

After four and a half hours of driving we had to stop for a break. I didn't want to fall foul of the police at this stage of the journey!

The trip down was very uneventful. The truck and trailer behaved fantastically. We collected the digger bucket without any delays and made very good time to Dover.

I turned to Sue. "Well that's been a pretty good run." Oops, I had spoken too soon. We saw a mass of red lights in the distance at the roundabout at the bottom of the hill into Dover. Oh no! Operation Stack was in operation following a fire in the Channel Tunnel. To add to the problem we had little fuel left and Sue was bursting for the loo! We crawled through the mayhem for 2 ½ hours. Finally, we checked in and boarded. What a relief, in more ways than one.

Once on board we made our way to the truckers café area for discounted food. Every little helps! It's very expensive for an HGV return ticket on the ferry. We had a passable chicken and chips meal. One bonus of the truckers' area is that you don't have to endure noisy kids running about or playing their iPods! Truck drivers just want to relax.

# Running on fumes of stress

We docked at Calais just after midnight with our fuel gauge on the red. Of course, everywhere was closed and not a soul about. Sue got angry with me, but what could I do.

Driving around looking for a petrol station is no fun when you are close to running out. The air in the cab was getting thick. A few cross words would be putting it mildly.

As we headed back to Calais port on another road in the hope of finding a fuel station, we couldn't help but notice a large number of people hanging around parked trucks. Presumably these were immigrants trying their luck for a ride to England - where the streets are paved with gold, so they are told. As we passed them, one or two looked straight at us. Their eyes had a look of pleading desperation. Clutching plastic bags that must have contained all their worldly goods you would have to be heartless not to feel for them. It's a sad state of affairs and I would do exactly the same if it meant it was the only way of providing for my family.

We finally came across some traffic controllers and got directions for an all night petrol station. What a nightmare, we were running on vapour! We got filled up and headed back out of Calais and south towards Paris.

It was now so late that our planned stopover time was way in the past. So we decided to carry on with our journey. I wasn't feeling tired.

I suppose the excitement of getting to our little bit of France kept me going. Anyway, we would see how it went.

We got south of Paris in record time - that was a first. For four in the morning there was quite a lot of traffic. Trucks and cars were flying past. I don't know how they stay on the road. One juggernaught passed us on a bend at a reckless speed with just inches to spare between us.

We drew closer to Orleans and stopped at a service station to fix yet another blown rear light. I also needed the loo. I went into the empty toilets. I heard laughing voices and footsteps approaching behind me. Then, suddenly, someone kicked the door. When I came out the two idiots were laughing and making fun. I shouted quite a few choice cockney words in their faces. I was tired and very angry. If I had had something heavy in my hand I would have wrapped it around their heads. They soon shut up. I went back to the truck and sorted out the lights on the trailer. I hate public loos!

We continued southward and reached a quiet Aire and parked up in the dark. I realised just how much we missed our motorhome as I climbed over the tools and bags in the rear box to retrieve our sleeping bags. We were now too tired to worry about where we would sleep so we both struggled into sleeping bags in the front of the truck and zonked off into dreamland.

CRASH! BANG! CRASH! Mumble, mumble - in French.

I was awoken from a deep sleep by service men emptying the bins right next to where we had parked. We seemed to be in their way.....trust me!

I looked across to Sue. She was completely submerged in her sleeping bag. I called out to her and her head popped out. She looked just like Little Weed from The Flower Pot Men...she had a cheeky little girl smile and giggled away. This was most unusual for Sue that early in the morning. I couldn't believe it, she was in a good mood even though we hadn't had much sleep!

I waited for the men to move off and then gingerly climbed out of my cosy bag. It was a cold morning. "Blimey it's only 8 30am," I muttered. The place was deserted. I set up the inverter and put the kettle on while Sue got breakfast ready. We were still quite tired. Breakfast over, we had a wash in the toilets where the water was freezing. It shocked us back into life.

# Roller coaster ride

We get on our way making tracks southwards. The roads were very quiet so I set the cruise control to 90kph and got in the groove with the other trucks. Unlike British roads you can maintain a constant speed for tens of kilometres on the quiet and very long straight roads.

During our journey we reflected on the time back in April when we passed this way. Very strange feelings overcame me. No motorhome towing a car but a truck and digger. Were we really going to Cayriech to start work on our place. I turned to Sue, she felt the same. After being together for over 35 years we tend to have very similar thoughts and feelings. My thoughts were distracted when I got a text from the forum member in France asking if we were on our way with their digger bucket.

I was feeling very mischievous and almost sent a text back saying Who? What? Where? Do we know you? What digger bucket? But Sue stopped me. I could almost imagine the panic at the other end.

We had a simple travel plan to just head south and see how far we got before we got tired but within the legal truck driving limits. It was quite obvious that summer was over by the number of caravans and motor homes that were travelling in the opposite direction. They were mostly French, a few Dutch, but not a lot of British about. The weather was looking promising and it was getting warmer the further south we went, thank goodness for that as a tent was going to be our home for the next few weeks.

As we passed through the Limousin region the truck handles the hills with great gusto, unlike our fully loaded motorhome had! The journey seemed to be going quicker this time. The views from the top of the hills were fantastic and in the bright sunshine you could see for miles. Back in April it had been overcast, wet and dingy.

It was a very pleasant drive. Autumn was on the way and leaves were starting to fall. It's funny how we remember certain houses on the way. We passed comments like, "Couldn't live there. Look how close it is to the road. What a shame its such a lovely house." Forgetting at that moment that the house was there long before the thundering great autoroute way was carved through.

After stopping for lunch on an Aire we contacted the forum member to sort out a meeting point to deliver his digger bucket. We met at a Carrefour supermarket next to the autoroute. It was so nice to put a face to a name. We had a good chat before wishing him farewell and continuing our journey.

The time was approaching 5pm and we were close to Brive, so we stopped for the toilets and a cuppa at the services. A coach pulled in next to us. It was from Doncaster and full of Brits en route to Spain. We got talking to the driver and his wife. They were staying overnight in a hotel in Brive. I thought it would be a good idea for us to stay over as well so the coach driver gave me a couple of telephone numbers of hotels they regularly use. We only had a couple of hours drive down to Cayriech but it would be getting dark by the time we arrived and we didn't fancy putting up the tent in the dark. Besides we needed a good night's sleep in a proper bed and a nice hot shower.

We drove the short distance into the town. After several circuits of Brive commercial area and various autoroute junctions we found the hotel. I had reserved a room using the mobile phone but I hadn't thought to ask directions. Finally we were booked in and settled. We showered and went to the restaurant for a meal.

As usual all the dishes I fancied contained wheat flour (gluten) so I ended up having a steak. I was so glad it came almost raw as the bits that were burnt were tough as old boots. Sue, on the other hand, had a delicious chicken dish. Fed and watered we went to our room and bed for a good nights rest.

## Tip toe through the night

I suddenly woke in the middle of the night in a bit of a panic. I just had to check that the truck was okay. Under the tarpaulin were two stone cutters, chain saw, brush cutter, whackers, Sue's new bike and lots of tools. The hotel was across the road from a very large gypsy camp.

I quickly and quietly got dressed without disturbing Sue. I tiptoed out of the darkened room in my slippers and walked downstairs to the foyer. There was no one about and the electric doors were switched off. It was deadly quiet. I am a little deaf and talk or shout a bit loud, often without realising it. Just then I noticed a lady in the kitchen with her back to me. I called out to her and she jumped about seven feet in the air. I desperately held back a giggle. She didn't speak English but she understood that I wanted to go outside and that I needed to get back in again. As I walked through the car park I prayed that she had indeed understood what I had said. I didn't fancy spending another night in the truck. Sue on the other hand was snoring and hadn't even heard me going out.

I needn't have worried there was no problem whatsoever. Had it been the UK everything would have been gone by now, including the truck!

Back inside the hotel I crept into our dark room. I was completely disorientated. My new pair of CAT boots were lying on the floor in the hallway and I went flying over them. Déjà vu, or something like that. I caught the light switch with my elbow so the room was awash with light. That woke Sue, she shouted, "What are you doing? Where have you been?

You're getting paranoid about getting the truck broken into, get back to bed." She wasn't amused! Eventually we drifted back off to sleep.

A bright sunny morning presented itself and we awoke refreshed even after my little night-time trip! I opened the curtains. Our room overlooked the gypsy campsite where children were already up and playing. They looked so happy as they pushed each other around on an old battered metal trolley. They were going around collecting the rubbish bags and taking them to big bins by the gate. I couldn't help smiling at them and thinking how a simple trolley was keeping them amused. It was the sort of thing I grew up with but I just wondered how times had changed for most others with their many expensive over indulgent toys.

Another hot shower was had before getting ready for the final part of our journey
We made tracks. I did another circuit of the roads around Brive for good measure. By mistake, of course, as Sue happily pointed out! We finally got on the autoroute but only until we could find a countryside Aire to stop for some breakfast. There would have been no point in eating at the hotel when all they can offer is croissants and toast that contained gluten!

# Relaxing with nature

Once again we appreciate and make use of the Aires around all of France's roads. It never ceases to amaze me what an abundance of wildlife frequents these parking areas. The clever creatures know there will always be food on hand. The finches are so cheeky, they literally fly up to you and ask for food. How could you resist them. A little wren darted about and a thrush tugged at a juicy worm. We watched the wildlife while we bathed in the early morning sunshine. Other travellers arrived. Taking a break, some walked their dogs, while others sat at the tables for some breakfast. The looming doom and gloom of Britain seemed light years away.

Time was getting on so we packed up and continued our journey to Cayriech. It was now only a good hour away. Like a repeat performance of our previous visit we drive through the tunnels that have been burrowed under the hills. They seem to reveal a secret garden at the other end each time we pass through. The light seemed brighter and the colours more vivid. There was just the odd tiny fluffy white cloud here and there in the clear blue sky. We were now entering the Tarn et Garonne. It was becoming so familiar to us. There was a little traffic but it was very peaceful at the same time. The temperature was rising as each kilometre passed. The air was warm and clean and wrapping around us. There were panoramic views all around us. What a wonderful place. It felt very comforting to be here – maybe it was home after all.

# A stones throw from Cayriech

I was in a dream world with the truck on autopilot. The silence was broken by Sue shouting, "Don't we get off here?" I had almost missed the turn for Caussade - known as the hat town and made famous by Maurice Chevalier and his straw hats. We gave a cheerful "Bonjour" to the lady in the péage kiosk and made our way around the ring road. We would normally go through the town but it's restricted for HGV's.

Half way round we noticed that a development we had seen back in April had taken shape in the form of a brand new Super U hypermarket. We looked at each other in surprise. "That went up quickly," commented Sue.

Maize was still standing in the fields as we passed the many little farms on the way to Cayriech. We noticed small changes. A couple of houses were building new garden walls in Monteils, a suburb of Caussade. Autumn obviously hadn't hit this area yet. As we drove the smooth winding road towards Cayriech the tall plane trees lining each side of the road were still in full leaf. They created a huge cathedral arch where they met with the bright sunlight flickering through and creating a strobe effect. It was lunchtime so there wasn't a soul about except for a couple of cars following us as we slowly made our way.

It never fails to tickle me when we pass the last house on the left as it is named Le Tourniquet. It conjures up all sorts of scenarios in my head.

We reached the last long right hand bend before our turn off for Cayriech with a mixture of apprehension, excitement and wonderment hitting me all at once.

As we drive down the lane we scoured the surrounding fields to see what was growing. It's quite narrow just here and we had to pull over to let a car pass by. As we headed down the hill we got a glimpse of the village through the trees. We reached the little bridge across the River Le're I slowed to almost a stop and peered over the low wall.

The water was very low. I thought of our campsite friends Remy and Jocelyne they would be very surprised to see us.

Nothing much had changed since our last visit back in April. The medieval buildings looked beautiful and well kept. There were flowers in bloom and the streets had been cleaned and tidied with pride. I continued on to the T junction next to the church. We couldn't help but notice the tiny cemetery opposite. The graves with their polished marble head stones reflecting like mirrors were adorned with flowers in planters. Like most French cemeteries it was very well kept. We turned right out of the village. It was very hot by now and there were lots insects buzzing around.

# Worrying news

50 metres short of the campsite we parked on the roadside and walked up the drive. Not a soul about. Then we spotted Jocelyne, she was indeed surprised, and very pleased, to see us. She was even more surprised to see the truck and digger instead of our motorhome. She speaks a little English and we explained that we needed a pitch for the tent. She was flabbergasted!

We asked where Remy was and she explained that he was at a clinic in Caussade having exploratory tests. We were a little concerned as it had been a very difficult year for the family. It was just a year since their twenty one year old son had died in tragic circumstances. Remy's father had also died the month before. Remy, apparently had been getting concerned that we had not been to start work on the mill. We needed to begin before the 21st of September, just a few days away, otherwise we would lose our Permis de Construire (building permission) forever. He had been making himself ill worrying. On top of that the campsite was losing money and bookings were down. It really wasn't fair as he had worked so hard and had so much bad luck and he was such a lovely man.

Jocelyne showed us the tent pitches. We had a choice of almost the whole site as there were just a few French and Dutch campers remaining. I went back to get the parked truck and trailer, I drove down to the pitch, unhitched the trailer and started unloading,

It was 27° - phew! Still, I was glad it wasn't raining and cold like the UK.

Last on, first off, there was method in my madness back in the UK I thought as I lifted the tent off the truck.

I had had a dry run back in the UK. Our £79.99 Aldi tent went up well, so I reckoned on having it up and finished in less than an hour…..1 ½ sweaty hours later I was still struggling. It was up…it was down again…what was going wrong? It was not like me to have these problems. Finally I got it to stay up. "Where's the door?" I asked Sue. "Round here," she replied. "How long has it been there?" I asked. "About an hour," she muttered. "Bollocks you're joking! It should be round here, no wonder it keeps falling over." I looked around to see if anyone was watching, or worse, taking a video for You've Been Framed or Youtube. All clear, no one about!

We walked the tent round leg by leg. Now totally knackered, I finally got the tent sorted and most of the camping stuff off the truck. I collapsed in a sweaty heap on the grass. We got a few curious looks from the remaining campers but they still gave us a cheerful, if slightly smirking bonjour.

Jocelyne called by before leaving to collect Remy from Caussade. She said she wouldn't tell Remy we had arrived so it would be a lovely surprise when they returned.

We hoped he was ok!

# All is well

I had just finished blowing up the double air bed when two smiling faces approached and called out to us. It was Jocelyne and Remy and we were so pleased to see his big grin. We all greeted each other, Remy kissed Sue on each cheek, I gave Remy a hearty handshake and a hug for Jocelyne. I am not into this kissing lark yet. I'm a cockney not a Frenchman. They explained the pains that Remy was getting was down to stress, worry and sadness and who could blame him. A lot of people would have thrown the towel in for less.

We had a good catch up with Sue helping me a lot with my French words. They were very pleased we had come to start work on the mill. Jocelyne admitted that Remy had said almost every day, "Where are the Kings? They should be here." We told them we were going to our local Probat builders merchant to pick up a sign to erect at the mill tomorrow. This was required by French building law before work could start.

It started to get dark so they said good night and left us to get settled in. The temperature was dropping but luckily I had brought our radiant heater. After some food we decided to go to bed, even though we hadn't been to see the mill, we needed to rest.

The Moulin has seen better days

# Dingle dangle

Sue went to bed first. We had separate sleeping bags and I had to climb over Sue to get to my side of the airbed. Now, you have to understand we haven't slept on an airbed before. I was naked and I had to adopt a crab like stance and slowly climb across on all fours. As I put my feet and hands on the airbed it sunk in four different directions at different times which had an opposite effect on Sue. She ended up bouncing and flopping about before she burst out laughing at my dangly bits hanging around while I tried to get onto my side of the bed. I finally made it. I flopped down and Sue bounced up. I wriggled into my sleeping bag. It was going to be a long night....

After what seemed to be just a minute or two of sleep we both woke up feeling cold. Sue had to go to the loo, we had a new porta potty which was in the next compartment of the tent. As she got up I rolled into the centre of the airbed. Now I was trapped in the sleeping bag. When she came back I then wanted to go as well. She says I drink too much tea! Afterwards, of course, I had to go through the whole process of getting back into bed. Again Sue bounced about and we just couldn't stop laughing. We had finally got settled when we heard a mosquito buzzing around our ears but we were too tired to do anything about it and anyway it was like an assault course trying to get up.

We must have both drifted back off to sleep. The next thing I knew was that I woke up with a dead leg and arm. I was trapped in the sleeping bag again and with Sue lying over me we were in a tangled heap in the centre of the now deflated airbed. The sides of the bed still had some air in them so we were sort of wrapped in a giant marshmallow. What a job we had getting up. After a whole lot of huffing and puffing I eventually discovered it was easier just to roll out onto the floor into another heap. We didn't seem to get much sleep and just couldn't stop laughing.

# Natures chorus

Dawn had broken. One thing about living in a tent is that you are near to nature. No, I will rephrase that, you are very near to nature! First the cockerels started calling to each other, which started the dogs barking and the dogs started the donkey braying. After all the kerfuffle it all went quiet. Then the dogs barked at each other again, which started the cockerels off, which started the donkey off. Next, a pair of doves might as well have been in the tent with us. They cooed loudly from their perch in the tree above us and to top it all a magpie started up. But the magpie had a split personality because he also thought he was a duck. He would get fed up with chattering and started to fly around quacking. What a racket! "I think I may as well get up," I said to Sue. But you just had to laugh!

By now it was 10am and the sun was filtering through the trees that lined the camping area. The rays created pockets of warmth and I moved about to stand in them. The sun was rising fast. It was going to be another lovely day.

We had planned on getting an early start as we needed to visit the Intermarché, the nearest supermarket but getting ready and having breakfast seemed to be going at a slow pace. By the time we had finished it was lunchtime - so we had lunch! Easy.

We eventually made it to the supermarket and to Probat for the sign, later in the afternoon. The manager at Probat remembered us from our visit back in April and gave us one for free as we would be opening a trade account with them. Shopping over we made our way back to Cayriech. That was after a few curious looks from other shoppers and drivers as the truck was still loaded with all the building gear and ladders.

Once back I set the compressor up to re-inflate the camp bed and inflate the extra double airbed as well. Sue thought one on top of the other would be better as we would be higher off the ground and all that. We would see!

Sue had another bright idea and zipped the separate sleeping bags together to make one double so we should keep each other warm. I set up the satellite TV and other bits of kit while Sue prepared some food. We had a nice quiet night in with a bar of chocolate in front of the telly and fire.

I ventured outside the tent before going to bed. It was a beautiful clear night, a still, crisp chill to the air and the stars were shinning brightly. It was so peaceful. Unlike our place in Yorkshire with the constant drumming from the M1 motorway, that was close by, at all hours.

Time for bed or should I say time for a game of Twister! Sue got in first then I crabbed over and wriggled in. Sue just burst out laughing. At least my dangly bits put a smile on her face, but not for the right reason. I lay there settled but Sue decided to turn over and pulled the sleeping bag with her. This in turn rolled me over towards her. I was now up very close to her and she got hot - menopause and all that! Suddenly she unzipped and flung the bag off as much as possible. By this time I was freezing my not so dangly bits off. It was going to be another long night!

The dawn chorus woke me up. We had had a cold restless night. We were going to have to buy an extra duvet. Yet another slow start to the day but after the long journey down from Yorkshire we had a much needed rest.

A trip into Caussade proved to be fruitless. We found one very expensive duvet which we didn't buy. We had several spare ones back in Yorkshire and I had looked at one on the motorhome bed before leaving for France - and left it behind. Did I need to bring it with us.....Yes. You plonker, I thought to myself. Too late now!

Sue with the little sign!

## Discovering a jungle

We went back to the campsite. The Mairie would be opening in a few minutes so we strolled down to the office in the hot sun, grasping the huge sign and Permis papers. As luck would have it the Maire was in the doorway ready to greet us. What a nice man he is, and his secretary too. They both took great delight in helping us to fill everything in, including writing on our sign.

We had a lovely chat about the coming meetings to discuss traffic and various other aspects of the village. He was proud to show us the plans. All changes for the better he assured us.

We said our goodbyes and left the beautiful medieval office which is attached to the church and adjacent to the Roman washing baths. So much history. We took a short walk through village. Flowers were still in bloom. A spectacle of colour from the abundance of flowers neatly planted in every conceivable area. Terracotta pots filled bright red geraniums lit up like giant flames against seven white stone steps that lead to a distressed wooden door, the colour of verdigris of une maison ancienne.

The scent streamed through the air of a wild climbing rose, dusky pink in colour with a lingering sensuous aroma. It was beautiful here and so peaceful.

We passed the ducks and geese they were too busy sleeping in the sun to even give us a glance. Normally they would make a fuss.

We turned left up our dusty white limestone track. The sun on the track was reflecting heat back at us. Phew! My heart was pounding with excitement. There was now a slight warm breeze blowing across the tall maize that towered above us. It caused a gentle swaying Mexican wave as each breath of air passed. In the distance we could see things were growing in our field - boy were they growing! As we drew closer we could see plants, about six feet high, full of berries similar to elderberries, multiplying it seemed before our very eyes. Self set trees had shot up. No idea what they were. Some areas that we had cleared back in April had turned into a forest of tall nettles and other spiky stingy things. " We won't be able to get anywhere on the land like this." I said to Sue. We left the sign near our gate and we looked over at the jungle before us. We had some work on. One thing for sure we have very fertile land.

We decided to make a start clearing a way through tomorrow. We returned to the campsite where we stayed for the rest of the day getting some relaxing time in the sun.

We had another night of disturbed sleep and dawn awakening. We lay in the tent listening to every little tweet, bark, croak and rustle in the undergrowth around the tent. When a dog barks we can almost pinpoint which house it belongs to. One dog seemed to be kicked out then constantly yapped and whined until it was let in again. It certainly didn't like the cold mornings.

A lazy start once again, even though I wanted to get on with the land clearing. We seemed to have lost several hours somewhere on our journey over from England.

The early morning sun was a welcome sight after all the bad weather we had had in the UK. I started my bread maker at 6am under torch light. I was looking forward to hot gluten free bread and a cuppa for breakfast and I wasn't disappointed. I sat back and relaxed in the sun and took my time over a couple of hot, thick slices with lashings of butter and a big dollop of marmalade. Even though we were in a tent, bringing some home comforts with us was vital. Sue was still in bed. She said I disturbed her sleep through the night but every time I woke up she was snoring in my ear! I put some of the extra covers over her that Jocelyne had loaned us. She turned, curled up like a cat and went back to sleep.

After a refreshing shower, I was going to make a start clearing the land.

I walked up to the campsite parking area and called out a cheery "Bonjour" to a French lady and, I think it was, her Dad - but you don't ask do you! They were in the next pitch opposite and camping in a tourer. Bonjour monsieur they replied.

Ambling down the white rocky footpaths, so bright from the sun's reflection, I was greeted by Remy, who was tending his much loved gardens, with the sight and scent of the multicoloured flower borders, it was a stunning picture, he waved and shouted, "travail." I laughed and replied, "Oui."

I climbed into the truck, the hot sun had turned the cab into an oven but before I could get both windows opened I started to melt, but it's better than the cold, I thought.

Turning left out of the campsite high up in the cab, I got a good view of the park opposite with the many newly planted trees with their little plaques giving details of each child and family from the village that had planted them. As I approached the village, barely getting out of second gear, I could see that the village gardeners were busy. I called out "Bonjour" and one replied, "le Moulin - beaucoup de travail," with a big smile. "Oui, beaucoup de travail," I replied and laughed. They waved as I passed. The friendliness warmed my heart.

As I drove the short distance to the mill my eyes were like the shutter on a camera, taking snapshots of the architecture, how each stone had been laid and what type of joint was used for the colombage balcony above the Mairie. My mind was acting like a hard drive storing random pictures for later use.

Reaching the end of the village I turned left up the track for the first time in the truck. It made me think back to my childhood. I would always get excited when going exploring somewhere new or being the first to leave footsteps in fresh snow. As I approached the mill, sitting high up in the cab, I was able to get a better view of just how much work we had in front of us. I stopped the truck at the gate and the hiss of the air brakes caused a cloud of white dust as it broke the silence. I climbed out of the truck and looked around. I heard myself saying, "Well this is it, our little Moulin"

It was so peaceful. There were birds singing and I could hear the river but only faintly so it must be low I thought. I got to work clearing a space with my machete so that I could erect the sign.

Sometime later Sue turned up on her new bike. She got cracking with the large croppers while I tackled the jungle with the brush cutter. Within a couple of hours we had cleared everything from the gate to our canal bridge. The temperature was rising fast. I decided to go over to the river for my first look during this trip. I still get excited wondering what I might see.

I had to tread a path through six foot high nettles! My legs had plenty of protection but the nettles sprung back and hit me in the face, ears and arms. Blimey did they have a sting in them! Undeterred I battled through to the river. It was indeed quite low. I could clearly see the deep pools between the water falls. We had our own natural piscine. It was then that I had the idea of making a plage with a little jetty and a bit of decking over some gravel and sand. I could just see myself sitting in a deck chair, with a cup of tea, watching and listening to the river as it cascaded over the falls.

My little dream over, I walked back to where Sue was still busy moving brambles and cursing as they caught her arm. I got to work erecting the sign and then took some photos. It was now way past midday and very hot in the bright sunlight. The area between the mill and the grange is a nice suntrap but with very little breeze. We decided to return to the campsite for a rest but we made plans to return later with the digger ready for stripping back the topsoil.

## Restless legs

Back at the campsite, we had a text from our friends in the UK asking if Bill and Min had arrived in Cayriech yet. Bill & Min are long term residents on the campsite. They were driving up from Spain and would be staying while Peter and Eileen made their way over from Lancaster to meet them. I broke into Goon mode doing an impression of the characters. I got a strange look from the French couple on the next pitch. I tried to explain the British comedy radio show to them. Blank faces all round until I mentioned Peter Sellers and then jumped into Inspector Clouseau mode. "Ahhhh!" they smiled. We all had a good laugh.

We settle down for a late lunch of fresh crisp salad. We decided to have a French two hour lunch break. So there we were, not a care in the world, sitting in the sun greeting a couple of straggling campers who were squeezing out the last bit of their summer before returning to Northern France or Holland. I thought I recognised the Dutch chap. He had been at the site back in April. He was a cheerful chap and you couldn't miss him as he was so tall and he towered above me. He remembered us and he was curious about the mill and what we had planned for the rebuilding.

A half hour had passed very quickly but I was getting restless. My leg was twitching and I was eyeing up my truck and digger keys on the table. Sue caught me looking. "Can you ever relax? You're driving me mad." I took a deep breath. "I am relaxed, no problem," I said. Oh yes! Who am I trying to kid? There was nothing for it. "I've got to get started before it gets dark," I muttered. Any excuse! I made my way over to the truck and hitched up the trailer. I waved to Remy and Jocelyne as I made a wide sweeping left hand turn out of the campsite and over the speed bumps to the end of the village. I had to reverse up the dusty track to the mill so that I could get the digger off the trailer.

The powerful Paccar engine had no trouble shoving the 3 ton digger and the fully loaded truck. I must have disturbed the neighbours with the loud beeping of the reversing warning echoing around the valley. In no time at all I had unstrapped my CAT, dropped the heavy ramps and reversed the digger off. Sue cycled down soon afterwards. It was the first time she had seen me drive the digger. I made short work of clearing an area for the tower scaffold and other building equipment.

After a couple of hours I had cleared from the gate to the bridge and moved the soil into large heaps ready for loading onto the tipper. It was now getting a bit late for making a noise and I didn't want to upset any neighbours. As we readied to finish off and pack up for the night Remy cycled down to the mill to see how we were doing. It was so nice to turn off the engine. The silence was deafening! My ears were ringing.

As usual, a simple question between Remy and myself turned into arm waving, sounds like, similar to - well you know what I mean when neither of us speak each other's language. But we got there in the end with a lot of laughs. Thankfully Sue was able to give me lots of words but, like most times, it was in one ear and out the other!

I put all the security into place, hitch lock, padlocks and chains on the equipment, the main digger boom resting on the back of the trailer, the 5 foot ditching bucket covering up the 2 foot bucket under the weight and the new satellite GPS GSM alarm set to maximum vibration detection and the perimeter set to 50 metres. I wasn't going to make it easy for any thieves. Remy was amused with all the contraptions. I explained how necessary it was in the UK. He remarked that gypsies were also a problem in these parts. Bugger! That was something I didn't want to hear. I closed the makeshift wire gate and I jumped into the truck and made my way back while Sue and Remy followed on their cycles.

# Alarming nights sleep

Back at the campsite, Sue was weary and didn't feel like making a meal. As luck would have it, Remy was cooking for other campers. The special tonight was Toulouse sausage, haricot beans and chips. We placed an order and I grabbed a quick shower. In no time at all it was ready and served with a "Bon appétit" from Remy. We settled down in the tent in front of the telly, with the heater switched on, we tucked into a bon repas. The large sausage, curled right round the plate, a large bowl of chips and an even bigger bowl of beans was all washed down with a glass of wine or two.

Time for bed and I felt a bit amorous; well I had had two glasses of wine! I didn't realise what a marathon it was going to be! First the onslaught of the double decker air beds that seemed to want to go in opposite directions. It wasn't the easiest platform from which to engage in marital cavorting. Suddenly my pillow disappeared off the end of the bed, quickly followed by my head. Then my leg dropped off the side. I seemed to be having difficulty in hanging on. There were no bracing points - I think the technical term is purchase! Everything seemed to want to go in a completely different direction to the one I wanted. Sue, on the other hand, was creased up laughing hysterically. She had had a glass more than me!

Finally we settled down. "God knows what the neighbours must think. They must be hearing every noise," I muttered, which started us both off laughing. We took deep breaths and calmed down. At the crucial moment

I got cramp in my left leg. I was in a very awkward position - like I said it's not easy on an air bed! I gritted my teeth. Sue, however, was completely oblivious to my plight. I couldn't spoil it for her. Like a true Brit with a stiff …………………upper……….. lip…...….sorry!

I bet you though, way hey hey!

I carried on despite the cramp in my leg giving excruciating pain. Thank goodness things were over. I bounced out of the bed, Sue bounced up and down and I rubbed my leg vigorously to get the circulation moving. Sue almost fell out of the bed laughing. The earth didn't move for me - but the bloody bed did!

After all the excitement, or not, we got off to sleep.

Our deep sleep was suddenly broken at 1.30am by a loud ringing tone. It was a text message - DIGGER ALARM SHAKE ALERT. I catapulted myself out of bed. Sue bounced about as I leapt over her. I stumbled around in the dim light from the mosquito zapper as I looked for something to put on. Ah, boxers, a tee shirt and moccasins. I can't find the zip end to the mosquito net. Finally I got out and grabbed a torch. The usual frantic search for my keys began. Sue groaned, "Where did you have them last?" "If I knew that I wouldn't be looking for them," I exclaimed. I was getting frantic now, throwing things in the air as I looked underneath bits of clothing laid around. Powerful beams of light were flashing around from my flood light torch as I searched. Then, suddenly I remembered. I grabbed my digger keys from inside my work boots – where else!

With torch in hand I needed something heavy to take with me. The only thing I could find was a spare tent pole. I jumped on Sue's bike - mine was still in bits. It was freezing cold. I must have looked like a madman. I was in the dark, racing down the hill through the village to the mill. I imagined a posse of gypsies making off with my digger. How on earth was I going to stop them with a tent pole?

My heart was pounding. I would sort out the bastards, they weren't getting my digger, I said to myself. I peddled like a seasoned yellow jersey holder. I hit the first speed bump and left the ground, while still whizzing through the village I hit the last speed bump with just as much force. I was launched into the air even higher - big mistake! I was now airborne at a fair speed and I had to turn left up the dusty track. I realised I couldn't pull on the brakes because I was clutching a big floodlight torch, a bunch of keys, a tent pole and the handlebars. I just made the turn by sliding the back wheel in the gravel. Phew, that was close! I bounced along the track to the gate of the mill. No lights, no vans and no sight of any gypsies.

Bloody false alarm!!!!

Nonetheless, I searched about flooding the whole area with light from my torch. I had never been down here at this time of night and it was so quiet you could have heard a pin drop. The red blinking indicator in the digger cab showed that the Tracker alarm had gone off. I reset it and had one last check. I turned around and made my way back to the campsite, praying all the way that no one in the village had seen me.

I climbed back into bed and Sue flopped about as I displaced the air in the bed. "False alarm. I am freezing cold," I said. "Don't you dare put your cold feet on me," Sue protested and we drifted back off to sleep.

Watercolour of Sue's Victorian tea room and gift shop

by Kim Prior

# Nature is amazing

What a contrast this Sunday morning was here in France to the last one we had back in Yorkshire. We were living virtually outside with the elements, nature and the fresh air. The sun was just rising and casting rays of light across the tent. There were birds singing, dogs barking, other noises that we couldn't quite make out. The odd tractor passed by. There were farm smells wafting through the air. Not unpleasant ones though. Healthy ones, we tried to convince ourselves.

"I'm hungry," I exclaimed. All the fresh air had given me a huge appetite. I got up and battled my way out of the zipped mozzie net. Yes. We still had mozzies! Sue had seven big eruptions on the back of her neck and the itching was driving her mad. I had splattered the little bugger the other night with a flip flop. It had taken some doing in a tent. It had probably looked a bit bizarre from the outside. A shadowy naked figure prancing about beating a tent to death from the inside and shouting, "Die you bastard die!"

I stood in front of the radiant heater. We had to leave it on all night now as it was getting towards zero at night. That was pretty chilly in a tent. So I warmed my freezing clothes before putting them on. I am driving Sue mad by making comments and muttering - it must be an age thing! "Brrrrrrrr! Gordon Bennett. Chilly willy. Brass bloody monkeys this morning." Then another "Brrrrrrrr! Cuppa tea Pete? Yes Dud." My interminable impressions of Peter Cook and Dudley Moor. "Shut up.

You've got verbal diarrhoea," Sue muttered. She turned over and tried to get back to sleep. I ventured outside and put the kettle on. I just love a cup of tea. Sue, on the other hand, has nettle tea. Yuck! Sue turned over for a lay in.

I looked around. It was very quiet apart from the occasional dog barking and the magpie flying about chattering with the odd quack, quack thrown in, it's a silly bird. The donkey and the doves could be heard in the background. Yes it was very quiet, only gentle natural sounds to be heard. That silence was broken by the whistle of the kettle on the stove. I whipped it off quickly before it got to a high pitch, I didn't dare to disturb Sue.

It was only 8 o'clock and I had finished breakfast already. I just can't lay in. I decided to put my bike together - well, the wheels and handle bars. It was easier to transport like that. I could hear Sue complaining about my tinkering. It's not easy to be quiet with spanners. Sue gave up and got up. Impossible to ignore my annoying habits. More tea and Sue was finally ready.

The sun was out again. We were having wonderful weather. I hoped it would last for the whole of our stay!

We made our way down to the mill on our bicycles. I tucked my walking stick under my arm just in case Remy's mum's horrible dog was on the loose. Whenever it saw me it would go for me. Perhaps I shouldn't have poked it in the eye with my stick during my last visit. It was self defence though!

A couple of minutes pedalling and we were at our gate. Sue still had to do a bit more clearing while I checked to see how high the digger bucket could reach toward the gable end of the mill. We will have to demolish it as we are extending at that end.

It's reach was good but not at a safe distance even in an enclosed cab. I could push the stone into the mill but that would make the job messy. There was no other thing for it but to erect the scaffold tower and remove the top section by hand.

I got the tower erected and Sue had done her bit of clearing. The temperature was slowly rising. Being a Sunday we didn't want to make too much noise.

While we were packing the tools away Sue noticed two large eagles circling very low above us and calling that echoing shrill whistle sound.

What a magical moment. With a few turns they caught the thermals and in the blink of an eye they were gone. We looked at each other in amazement.

We closed the wire gate and glanced at the mill, "We'll soon get it sorted," I said to Sue with a sound of optimism in my voice. On our way back through the village I noticed the bloody dog. I told Sue to go first on the other side of the road. It spotted me and made a dash for me but with a bit of nifty sprinting I out ran the horrible thing.

At the campsite Bill and Min had arrived from Spain. We left them to get settled in and relaxed for the rest of the day. We decided to get an early night as Monday would be the start of proper full time work on the mill.

# Demolition men

In the early hours another loud ringing tone and DIGGER ALARM SHAKE ALERT shattered the night air. I was ready this time so with proper clothes and a weapon I raced down to the mill on my bike. All is quiet. Another false alarm. I had never had this problem before so I reset it and turned the sensitivity down. It was very dark. I heard a noise in the trees. The hairs on the back of my neck stood up and I started to imagine all sorts of things. The shadows created by my floodlight made me jump. "Bloody hell, pull yourself together," I said to myself. I locked the digger door, closed our wire gate and pedalled off down the track with a couple of wary looks over my shoulder. I must stop watching those vampire movies!

Back at the tent Sue was still sleeping. Well she was until I bounced over to my side of the airbed. "Another false alarm," I said and drifted off to sleep.

It was 4 am and I was wide awake. The excitement was killing me and I could not wait to get started on the mill. After all, that was what we were here for. I tried not to disturb Sue, which was pretty impossible in a tent. I carefully climbed over her causing her to bob up and down on the air bed. "What are you doing? What time is it," she muttered. "I don't know but it's bloody freezing," I replied. I warmed my clothes on the heater. The more I tried to be quiet, the more noise I seemed to make. The silence of the morning was interrupted by the zip on the door, the boiling kettle rattling on the stove, the stirring of my tea, the lid off the sugar jar dropping and clanking about. Even buttering my toast was echoing around the campsite! The other campers must have thought a mad man was on the loose! I could hear Sue groaning and complaining with every noise. I sat quietly in front of the heater but it's not easy eating crunchy nut cornflakes whilst trying to suppress the crunch!

After breakfast I made my way to the showers. Avoiding walking on the gravel paths I tiptoed like Wee Willy Winkie in the darkness. BANG, as the door to the shower block closed behind me. "Bugger." I stripped off, it was cold enough for freezing the balls off a brass monkey. I go for gold. As the powerful water jet hit me I jumped back and pinned myself to the wall, to try and avoid it. I sprung forward as the freezing cold tiles touched my back, I threw myself out of the cubical. It was the quickest shower on record! I got dressed with teeth chattering. Sod the noise, I ran back to the tent on the gravel path to get in front of the heater.

By now it was 6 am and time to go. I walked up to the truck and tried to set off quietly, yeh! Who was I trying to kid. The powerful engine and turbo kicked in and I roared out of the campsite and down to the mill.

At the gate it was very silent, even the larks were sleeping. I turned the truck towards the gable end of the mill, switched to full beam and pointed my 24v flood to where I was going to work. Gloves on, club hammer, chisels and crowbar in hand I climbed up to the top of the scaffold tower. I looked over towards the village. I hope they can't hear me I thought to myself.

Demolition in the early hours isn't the quietest of jobs. As bits of rubble fell they hit the aluminium tower which sent loud rings across the valley. It was almost like playing a tune as different bits of scaffold were hit by even bigger lumps of stone. I looked around to see if any lights had been turned on, or an old French lady with a rolling pin was making her way across the field to batter me. I was in luck. Everyone was still sound asleep.

From the top of the tower I got fantastic views of the surrounding area. Dawn was breaking and the warm glow illuminated the distant horizon. The birds started singing. I climbed down from the tower picked up my flood light and made my way over to the river. As I got close a huge heron took flight. It was like the launching of Concorde. It flew up river and disappeared in the darkness below the canopy of trees that line each side of the bank.

I just love wildlife and I wondered what I might find or see next. Playtime over I got back to work. It was just past 7am. I looked down from the tower as a familiar figure approached. It was Remy, the campsite owner, and he had gloves and work clothes on.

He explained that he had come to work with me. I was truly touched by his very kind gesture. So side by side we made short work of demolishing the heavy 70cm thick wall. We threw stone after stone into open spaces on the ground so we avoided damaging the stone faces as they could be re-used. Each stone hit the ground with a deep thud and left great indentations where they landed. As soon as we ran out of clear spaces we moved all the stones into piles up against the grange. Each pile was made by carefully separating them into similar size and type.

By 10 o'clock the sun was shining directly upon us. It was bright and very pleasant. It was then we found a couple of discarded snake skins. They were in the crevices of the wall. One was about a foot long and the other a similar length but a much bigger girth. The scales were so delicate. Remy exclaimed "Serpent" and I said "Snake". We had a chat, albeit very basic, about them. We both learnt new words with each of us trading one off the other. It's one way to remember! Just then Sue arrived on her bike. She was surprised to see Remy working with me. We all mucked in together shifting the stone - Sue keeping everything tidy.

By lunchtime we had demolished half of the gable and stacked the stone. Remy left on his bike and Sue followed on hers. I left a little later in the truck.

I called at Remy's house on the campsite on my way back. There I met Jocelyne and I explained as best I could that Remy was under no obligation to help. I felt guilty because I had helped him on the campsite and loaned him some tools back in April he might have felt he had to lend a hand. She explained that it was good for him to get away from the campsite and take his mind off all the bad things that had happened to them over the last year. It was good for his heart and his mind she told me. I felt sadness and humbled. That someone who we had only known for a short time would help us in this way was truly touching. Just then Remy came out. I asked Jocelyne to explain how much his friendship and help meant to me and how glad I was that in helping me it took his mind off the pain and sadness they had been going through. His eyes welled with tears. It was a very emotional situation. We said our goodbyes and went for lunch.

Not needing the truck, Sue and I cycled down to the mill for another stint. It was 25° and sunny. What fantastic weather for the time of year as it was raining back in the UK. We felt so lucky to be here and so glad we picked this part of France. We only had an hour for lunch as we were both eager to get back to work. A little later Remy returned with his usual cheerful "Bonjour." He worked very hard with us until 6 pm. Sue left earlier to prepare an evening meal. "It's a surprise," she said. I couldn't wait.

After a tidy up with my CAT excavator it was getting close to 7 o'clock so I packed up and cycled back to the campsite. As I drew close I got a faint whiff of curry. Had we got some new Pakistani neighbours? I didn't think so. It must be Sue, she knew how much I loved home cooked curry. I had a quick shower and we then sat in front of the telly with a lovely meal and a glass of wine. We relaxed for the rest of the evening until tiredness got the better of us, besides we just couldn't wait to tackle the airbed for another night of fun.

CAT makes easy work of clearing the land

# A windy night

The dawn chorus woke me at 7am, I was not sleeping very well on the airbed. I seemed to wake up feeling like I had gone ten rounds with Frank Bruno. It took some coming around even after several cups of tea.

After breakfast I trotted down to work at the mill. No sooner had I arrived than Remy turned up. I asked him the best that I could if he was neglecting the campsite. "Non," he replied, "Beaucoup de travail au Moulin." Well that was the bit I could understand.

We got to work demolishing the final section of the gable end. Sue arrived to help us stack the stone. Remy was surprised to see how hard she was working on yet another hot day.

We decided to have a typical French lunch so we made our way back to the campsite together. After a two hour lunch we went back to the mill. To our surprise Remy was already there and working. We were embarrassed but in a nice way. We couldn't thank him enough. He worked very hard. At the end of the day we returned to the campsite tired and hungry.

We had a catch up chat with Bill and Min. They had no definite plans but would be staying in Cayriech until Peter & Eileen arrived from Lancaster. Wishing them goodnight we realised we had lost track of the time. It was too late to cook or eat too much so we had beans on toast.

An hour later while watching the TV I felt stirrings. Something was brewing deep down. We were very tired as it had been a long day so we went to bed. After the performance of tackling the airbed we finally got settled. Just then a huge long loud fart erupted. The airbed seemed to amplify the sound. It must have echoed around the silent campsite. Everyone must have heard it.

Sue simply burst out laughing. As she did, another one, even louder than the last, just burst forth. Within minutes we were in hysterics. I clenched my buttocks to suppress the sound but it was just as loud albeit a higher pitch. We were now out of control. The laughing hurt our sides and the more I tried to hold back the worse things got.

After a few deep breaths we settled down only to start the whole process again. I always get the giggles at passing wind. I was in hysterics when I watched the film Blazing Saddles and Peter Sellers in Pink Panther and the outtakes in the lift scene.

God knows what the few remaining campers thought. It must have been a slow methane build up. The Toulouse sausage and haricot beans, then the curry and the balance had finally been tipped with beans on toast. What a windy night!

# Mind your head

The days were long and hot and to say it was peaceful would be an understatement. The whole experience was calming. The breeze through the trees, birds singing, insects busy buzzing around, the gentle noise of water cascading over the waterfalls.

The villagers seemed to go about their daily chores without a care in the world. Always a cheerful "Bonjour" and "Ça va?" Remy would often exclaim "Cayriech est Paradis" He had moved his immediate family down from Normandy for health reasons many years ago and I could see why.

We had to break off from work and have a rest in the shade. We were now taking the French two hour lunch breaks. They were certainly needed.

At the mill we were starting to make headway. We had stacked the large heavy stone into neat piles for re-use. We next had to move into the mill to clear the last 65 years of neglect. Old cart wheels, bits of oak from the grain collecting hoppers, oak floor and roof beams that had fallen in. Just to make things a bit more difficult we had found a pile of firewood that was stored behind the second mill stone. It was wedged in and buried by heaps of soil that must have blown in like the shifting sands of the Sahara.

The remaining gable end wall that was still standing seemed very precarious. I wasn't too happy about our safety if we were working below it, so I decided it needed to come down before we ventured into the mill. To clear it I drove the digger across le petit pont and up the steep bank to the rear of the mill. I got stuck in clearing all the vegetation and stripped the area back to bare soil. Eventually this area will be a covered terrace out from the kitchen. That was an advantage of having two levels of land around the mill.

I propped the ladder against the gable and told Sue and Remy to stand back in-case of falling stone. As I climbed the ladder, clutching a long 30mm thick rope, a large piece of stone, disturbed by the ladder, whizzed passed my ear. Sue shouted out, "Where's your hard hat?" Silly me and I am a stickler for safety on sites. I climbed to the top, hung over the gable and hooked a bowline over a large protruding piece of old purling support. A few pulls with the digger and the wall swayed back and forth. Then all of a sudden it fell all in one piece towards me and the digger.

I emerged from the safety of the digger cab surrounded by a huge plume of white lime dust and with a satisfied grin, I turned to Remy and said, "Pas de problème." Another huge pile of stone to stack, with that job done, we returned to the campsite for tea.

Before reaching our tent we were stopped by a fellow camper enquiring how we were getting on and another camper quizzed us about what we were doing. I suppose we looked a bit odd covered in dust and wearing work clothes and sometimes carrying tools. When we explained and showed them the drawings, we mostly received a look of surprise followed by a "Bon courage" or "Beaucoup de travail," always with cheerful encouragement and always positive.

Sue Shopping
Sunday market day at the beautiful historic medieval town of
St Antonin Noble Vale

## Treasure

Another hot and cloudless day, we made our way down to the mill, which we had nicknamed Kingsmill. (our surname being King) The French didn't seem to understand at first that we had a bread in England called Kingsmill and found it very amusing. After a lengthy discussion, they thought it even more bizarre with my allergy to wheat flour and gluten.

We made a start clearing the inside of the mill. Remy, yet again, turned up to help, we have never experienced this degree of kindness from anyone before but we have to remember his circumstances. I suppose we cheered him up and it was great fun for me trying to converse with him.

Whilst clearing some stone from the side of the mill Remy suddenly exclaims, "Trésor." We dashed over to him to see what he had found, it was a small, unrecognisable coin. We then got into a long conversation of sorts, about metal detecting. I waved my arm from side to side and made beeping sounds. Remy carried on by explaining where the French used to keep their money before banks were invented. He said even today, the old French don't trust banks. I wonder why?

He told us of a builder friend who found a tin full of Napoleon coins hidden behind a stone in a loft. We started to fantasise over what we might find on our plot that had been, to our knowledge, a working mill since the 1400's or before, when the church was built. Who knows, it was on a Roman road after all.

Later on we moved some very large stone steps with the digger and found some old glass calibrated bottles, a couple of very old and heavy hand blown crystal goblets that had been damaged and an old metal scale and weights. Not quite the treasure we had hoped for, but we told Remy that the real treasure was the mill and the location - what a find. He gave a big smile and agreed.

While Remy and I cleared and stacked the heavy stone Sue worked constantly keeping the whole site clean. As she swept up at the front of what was left of the mill entrance she uncovered a large round stone. Further cleaning and digging revealed we had another full size mill stone but this one was set in the floor. What a nice find.

The more rubbish we removed the more interesting the mill got. It was obvious that the mill had been extended at some time. We found an old doorway at the back that has been blocked up. Stone steps at either end of the large mill stones led underneath to the water below the arch. There an oak barrage was controlled by two timbers that came up through the arched roof. Perfectly square holes had been carved into the stone to control it. I noticed that one of the big stones had one curved side that faced south in the mill, for no apparent reason. Perhaps it was made to match the grange that has one south facing curved corner, we add these odd findings to our list for research.

With all the vegetation, beams and soil removed we were able to get better access to the two huge 170cm mill stones and the openings to the archway below. I climbed underneath to the mill base that had been carved out of an enormous rock. It formed the dam for the canal. In the base there were two deep round holes about 60cm in diameter. This was where the vertical turbines were fitted. We had found one intact and it was made of oak. It was just fascinating, and mind boggling, to consider the work that had gone into the construction all those years ago. And to think that it had all been done with just very basic tools. We did some research on Remy's computer and I found a similar example which was a Roman design that had been found at an archaeological dig. It just got more exciting by the day.

As the day progressed we had a surprise visit. Our friends Alan & Viv from Lalbenque called to see how we were getting on. That gave us an excuse to take a break from the heavy work. Alan was very interested in our finds. He so wished he had found an old mill, but certain types of property are getting few and far between.

They are building a new house on an elevated site about 20kms away to the north of us. He can visualise the enormous potential our place has albeit with a lot of hard work. But as I have said before, we are not renovating or restoring it is more like a new-build with original old materials and using modern building and insulation methods whilst keeping the mill's appearance and expanding on it - well that was the plan!

Alan insisted that when the time came to drain and dredge our canal he wanted to be on hand to witness the work. He was convinced that we would have some unusual finds. He could be right as I would think it hadn't been dredged for hundreds of years, so who knows what we may find. We walked around the land looking at the many trees and marvelled at the abundance of wildlife and insects. We were drawn to the noise of the river. The crystal clear water flowing swiftly, the deep pools between the waterfalls created small swirling eddies here and there.

On the far bank where the river had flooded earlier in the year it had made a small new channel, so on the edge of the field opposite we now had a back drop of mini waterfalls. Even the most talented landscape artist would be hard pressed to capture this natural paradise. The energy and movement gave our place a whole new dimension and it was a beautiful magnet for all types of creatures.

The long day over our friends said their goodbyes. Sue and Remy returned to the campsite but I decided to stay behind awhile and to make a new entrance and a road that would make it easier to get the tipper in, it would be easier to clear the huge mounds of soil, lime and rubble. Our existing entrance could be closed off to give us a courtyard and walled garden. I worked till it got dark and returned to the campsite on my bike leaving the truck behind.

Remy enjoying a change of jobs.
Camping proprietor to digger driver

Sue & Remy getting the very heavy stone steps ready for removal

# Buzzing around!

Later that evening I realised I had left the plans and my phone in the truck, so I decided to go and get them. I cycled down towards the village, the lane was very dark and quiet. In the distance the warm glow of light from the church made a definite line on one side but very dark towards the campsite. In complete contrast, the nucleus of the village was awash with glowing golden light - safe and inviting. It was 12.30 pm and the air was very still but with a chill that made me wish I had put a few more clothes on. The village at this time of night took on a whole new look. It was even more peaceful than during the day. The stillness and silence was even more apparent but it was warm and friendly at the same time. There was just a couple of slithers of light through the shutters on one of the houses.

I reached the end of the village and turned left up towards our track. I was now in complete darkness as I bumped along the newly dug road to the truck. I say road but it was just a clearing of vegetation and levelling of soil four metres wide. It was pitch black so I hopped in to the truck and put the headlights on, then climbed out and opened the side shutter to get the drawings. Just then I heard a very loud buzzing. I turned around but I couldn't see anything. I retrieved the drawings and phone then closed the side shutter. The buzzing got even louder and came from more than one direction. It seemed to be following me so I moved into the light of the truck.

To my horror a swarm of hornets, the size of small birds, were all around me. They migrated to the headlights. What do I do? I moved away and they followed me. Bugger! What was going on? I never expected anything like this at this time of night nor had I ever seen anything quite as big as these before. Something was attracting them but what? I stood frozen still while they bumped into the headlights of the truck. At least that was keeping them busy I thought. I would have to make a dash for it. I turned the truck lights off and made ready to cycle off but they suddenly came for me. It was then I realised I had my bright camping LED headlamp strapped to my head and still switched on. What a plonker! I hurriedly switched the truck lights back on and then switched off my headlamp.

With my bike in one hand I turned the truck lights off, slammed the door shut, jumped on my bike, peddled like crazy and shot off in the dark like a rocket. My heart was thumping. I didn't dare look back. Boy was I glad to be away from there! As I cycled back through the village I eased off and listened for buzzing. All was quiet thank goodness. When I got back to the tent I told Sue about my adventure and she had a good laugh at me.

# England beckons

In a couple of days we were due to leave for England. Sue had to get back to prepare her shop for Christmas which seemed to be getting earlier every year. We made good use of the hot sunny days to clear the area and tidy up. We loaded the digger onto the trailer and stowed the tools ready for our departure.

We stacked what we could of the last gable end that I had taken down. We left the rest of the stone lying in a heap of dust and rubble. Sadly it would have to wait for our return next year.

Our neighbour turned up and at great speed he cut the maize next to our place. In no time at all he'd finished and was moving across the road for the next field. His tractors and huge trailers ran back and forth to his farm carrying the animal feed maize. It looked like a bumper crop. We gave him a wave as we drove up through the village.

Back at the campsite Bill and Min called by to see how we had been getting on. I was still loading the truck parked next to the tent ready for leaving in the morning. The weather forecast had threatened rain but it held off for the rest of the evening.

We had the majority of all our camping stuff loaded up and were leaving just the basics out for our last evening meal in the tent. Time had just flown by. We fell into bed, bounced about and had a laugh. It would be the last time we slept on the airbeds - thank goodness.

Our slumber was disturbed late in the night by the sound of heavy rain. Perhaps it was telling us we should leave. We had been very lucky so far.

We were up bright and early. It was still drizzling. Not a good time for packing a tent away. Bill and Min said "Bon voyage" and went off shopping. They returned at lunchtime and are not in the least surprised to see us still there. True to form we were still packing. Where does all the stuff come from? A planned early start northward had passed. Other campers called by to wish us well. Everyone was so friendly.

Finally, we hit the road at 1.30pm. We headed out of the campsite bidding farewell to everyone, especially Remy and Jocelyne. We text our friends at Lalbenque to tell them that we were on our way home. We had our last look at the village as we passed through. The rain had stopped and the sun was shining brightly again. The night rain had cleaned the air to leave the village sparkling.

Over the little hump back bridge and one last sad look at the River Le're. The water was clear and glittering in the sunlight. Knowing that the river flowing below us had, just moments before, passed by our mill we gazed at each other and no words were necessary. Our thoughts turned to our long journey ahead.

Time had simply vanished. We didn't seem to have been there long enough. As we made our way towards Caussade the roads were quiet. The fields seemed to be giving a sigh of relief after the long dry spell. Suddenly a sad moment descended on me. I felt I was leaving home behind and on an unwanted journey.

As we circled our way around the Caussade ring road we looked across to the few builders' merchants on the way. We were glad of the research we had put in before we bought the mill. It was a major factor when deciding where we were to live. Being a builder and living miles from merchants was not an option.

We drove through the péage and onto the northbound autoroute just a few minutes from the town. There was no turning back now. I looked at Sue and said, "I don't want to return to the UK," but, as usual, we don't have a choice at the moment.

The autoroute down this way is very quiet. It's a fairly new road. It's very clean, unlike the motorways of Britain which can be strewn with litter and road-works. I set the cruise control, sat back and took in the views. The weather was now back to bright sunshine and we had to leave it behind. We stopped for a late lunch on an Aire just north of Cahors. We got some inquisitive looks from other travellers. I suppose we looked like gypsies.

# Ladies of the night

Our journey north was uneventful. Conversation was fairly sparse as we were feeling down. We made a stop near Orleans. The weather had changed and it was now overcast with drizzle which most definitely matched our moods.

We had made good time but as we hit the Paris outer ring road, suddenly the traffic stopped, the ring road was closed. Two and a half hours later we fought our way out of the mayhem and we get just north of the Charles de Gaulle airport totally exhausted. Satnav is no good when it's telling you the road you want is in a tunnel below you which is closed. I followed my nose in the end.

We pulled off at the large commercial area near the airport. We could see several hotel signs lit up in the distance. I noticed a couple of young ladies walking which seemed a bit odd in the circumstances - well to me it did. We were now very tired so I pulled up outside one of the automatic hotels where you just use your credit card to get a room. For some inexplicable reason I just couldn't get it to work.

A short distance away, at another hotel, I keyed in all the information and at last the screen said they had a room. I finally got it to accept the card and paid but I couldn't get entry to the building. I was getting very frustrated by now and even more tired. I pressed the help button and a cheerful young lady's voice said, "Bonsoir". Luckily she spoke a little

English, but she kept asking me where I was. I didn't know the name of the area. She finally tracked me down and explained that she was in a call centre somewhere in France. She gave me a door code and wished me good night. I must have missed something somewhere in my confused and extremely tired state!

We drove the truck and trailer around to the back parking area of the "U" shaped hotel. Our room was the last but one from the end. I was getting close to exhaustion so we grabbed our overnight bags and fell into the room. It was a type of maisonette entrance with WC, shower and tiny kitchen on the ground floor and bedroom on the first floor. It was very clean and comfortable thank goodness. After washing and checking that the truck was OK from the window, we fell onto the bed in the darkened very quiet room in a heap of confused exhaustion.

Dreamland seemed just a second away. But No!

Bang!        Bang!        Bang!        Squeak!        Squeak!
Oui…Oui….Oui….Yar…Yar…Yar…..

Oh no! Just our luck to have moved into the only room next to a courting couple - or something else. It certainly seemed the French and German relationship was being repaired in one way or another. We could not believe it. We suddenly both burst out laughing. What else could we do. In the middle of laughing Sue said, "If we can hear them, they must be able to hear us." That made us laugh until our sides hurt.

Suddenly it went quiet. We lay there, Sue whispering, "Thank goodness." The next second a mad rush of rapid banging, squeaking topped with lots of Oui's and Yar's and a almighty crashing sound! Then, all quiet again. It was over. But no. They started talking Five minutes later, thankfully, they both left in a car that was parked outside. So maybe the young ladies I saw strolling were ladies of the night. We drifted off into a deep sleep.

Our dreams were suddenly broken. We were completely disorientated in the darkened room. Where were we? Bang, Bang, Bang, Rattle, Rattle. What the bloody hell was going on next door? It was only 8am.
I looked out of the window. A repair van was outside and two workmen were working in the red light room next door. We got up, showered, had breakfast and loaded up to get on our way. One of the repair men said he was sorry for waking us. UGH! Perhaps they were repairing the bed!

# Almost on our way

The drive from just north of Paris went well and we made good time to Calais. "We should be home in Yorkshire at about nine," I said. When will I learn to keep my mouth shut!

No such luck. Arriving at the check-in at Calais we were told the French were blockading the ferries for something or other and they had no idea when we would be able to leave. We were then beckoned into a hanger for a complete inspection and checked over by UK Customs. Finally we got parked. Luckily we had food in the 12volt fridge and plenty of water. A British truck driver parked next to us said he was parked for 3 days last time. Nice to meet cheerful people!

We must have one of those faces, agony aunt or something, the driver parked next to us started to tell us his life story. His marriage breakup, his new teenage girlfriend and his love life, his secret cheap diesel for his lorry but we were sworn to secrecy and his run-ins with the French smuggling police. Needless to say he was stopped before he boarded the ferry. Customs seemed to be giving his truck a good going over.

News filtered through that the blockade was being lifted. We eventually boarded some 3 hours late. We had a subsidised meal in the trucker's café. It was late evening as we landed on UK soil and the roads were very busy. The M25 was mad and as we approached the Dartford Toll it was very clear we were back in the UK by the aggressive driving.

Driving north up the A1 we had planned on having a stop on the way for a sleep but all the parking areas were full so we did one last slog back to Barnsley and arrived home in the early hours.

I got Sue settled in the flat and gave our two cats a cuddle. I turned to Sue, "I am sleeping in the truck" and went back outside. No way was I going to leave a loaded truck outside overnight as I knew it wouldn't be there in the morning.

In the following months I had my almost full fuel tank siphoned, fuel locking caps broken off twice, my new ratchet straps stolen, and our site power tools stolen, Oh! And my wheelbarrow and shovel.

Oh, the peace and quiet of our little bit of France seemed so far away. Ah well, till the next time!

## Another year passing

It was an extremely busy time for us in the UK and the hectic life where we were just getting on with things as usual. So! It was decided! We just had to make a date for our next French digging trip. If we didn't do it now then time would just pass by and before we knew it Christmas would be with us again and another year gone. Our permanent move to France would be another year further away.

We debated the best time to leave the cold and damp Britain that we were so eager to get away from. I still had the winter blues and we needed something to look forward to.

The flat was very nice but it was still a flat with no proper outside space and in a busy, growing part of Barnsley. On top of that we were still down in the dumps as our planning application to extend our building in Barnsley was just not happening. So our escape to France and the building work to the rest of the flats was on hold.

We both agreed that the best time to set off would be the end of May or at least no later than the second week of June. Besides it would be getting warmer by then and our home once again was to be a tent. Even though Cayriech was a lot further south than Barnsley, the heart of freezing Yorkshire at that time of year, it could still be cold in the early mornings.

Learning from past mistakes – no, not really mistakes but everyday goings on that got in the way of life - I conditioned myself into believing that I would get everything ready at least a week before departure.

I had posted a message on the French forums that I would be travelling down to South West France and if anyone wanted anything brought over I would be only too happy to oblige. That was not for monetary gains. I know only too well how it feels when you use a carrier to transport something from many miles away and you just hope it arrives in one piece. With me bringing something down it is on a more personal level and I feel in some way helpful. There are some things you just cannot get or, if you can, you pay a small fortune for them in France.

A couple of forum members replied. One asked if I could get some bath trims from B&Q and the other if I could transport some field gates and posts. The price of gates from the UK were very favourable but the transport cost to France was not. The six foot gates arrived just in time for me to load them on the truck. The bath trims were to be the finishing touch to a shower that had been out of use for months so I had better not forget them.

The three day drive down to Cayriech was going to be too much for Sue to endure again. The truck was a bit uncomfortable for long journeys so I booked a flight to Toulouse for her. So far so good, except I had to be in Cayriech a few days before her to get the tent set up and ship shape.

My plan was looking good but a week before my departure I got a telephone call from a client I had been advising. It was good news for him as his huge government funding had come through. I had been working on it for six months and now I needed to submit drawings to the planning department - just when I didn't need the pressure.

Burning the midnight oil and fitting every little job in was a nightmare. Loading up seemed worse than our last trip. Stuff has just vanished and to top it all Sue said we needed a bigger tent as we would be staying for at least six or seven weeks. I didn't even attempt to change her mind and take the tent from last year. I would have been wasting my breath she wanted a bigger tent and that was that!

Now, bear in mind, we now had to search out and find a tent. I also had to load the truck, get it serviced and inspected, complete the drawings, fill out umpteen bits of paper and forms - all in triplicate, so enough paperwork that would put a small wood in jeopardy - and visit a couple of camping shops to try out tents, hoping that whichever we decided on was in stock..

The planned departure day of Thursday came and went. I was still doing the drawings in between loading and other work. If I hadn't booked Sue's flight from Manchester for the next Week I would have given myself another week. But that is time for you, where does it go?

There was no way I could leave until Saturday. I gave a sigh of relief, well sort of, that gave me just a little more time. I had wanted to miss the bank holiday traffic hence the reason for wanting to set off early. The best laid plans and all that. Why bother I asked myself?

We finally found a tent that Sue liked and they had it in stock, but then we also started buying other stuff - big stuff for camping. New beds to replace the air beds we had last year, kitchen stuff, just more stuff. Any more stuff and I would have to change the 7.5 ton truck for a 32 tonner!

I was running out of time. I had to take my truck in at the last minute for its eight week Vosa safety inspection. The insurance commercial transport green card arrived in the post just in time. I didn't get stopped in Europe last year but you never could tell. I had a mental list of everything. I think mental was the right word. I was talking to myself, "Yes I am going mental."

I was getting stressed. I was running around like a blue-arsed fly and getting angry with myself for taking on so much. Then the plotter for the drawings stopped working. Great! I stormed about frantically looking for spare pens & ink. That's the trouble when you move from a very large house with offices and studio into a flat - you lose stuff because it's all in boxes. Stripping the plotter pens down was a messy business and I'm getting the evil eye from Sue. I got ink on the clean towels. I had to get the master drawings done before the weekend otherwise I couldn't get any copies produced. I just made it…phew!

Sue was shouting at me, "You've done it again. I don't know why we bother. You've left everything until the last minute again." I blurted out, "No I haven't."

"Yes you have. That's it, you can cancel the flight, I'm not going." Our two Siamese cats hate us shouting so they ran and hid. I kept quiet. I know my limitations. This was one argument I couldn't win. On top of that, Sue's stress levels were high with all my dashing about getting ready. Things calmed down, finally I collapsed into bed at midnight and went into a deep sleep.

# Plans finally come together

I was up at 4 am. Drawings finished, copies done, forms done. But I was still loading stuff and there were still things I hadn't done. I was keeping Sue awake despite trying not to make a noise. "You're driving me mad. I've got to work as well today."

It was now almost 6am. I crept out of the flat and drove round to the farm to collect the digger and trailer. Dawn was just breaking. I called into the milking parlour. Geoff had been milking since four thirty. He's a lovely bloke and very gentle, an old school farmer into organic farming and cares passionately about his animals. The farm was very quiet except for the shush, click sound of the vacuum pumps pumping the milk. The cows were mooing as if to say Ahhh! That's a relief off my udder. Cow Number 64, one of Geoff's oldest and most precious ladies, nudged the food hopper in the milking stall. She's a clever old girl. She knows exactly which stall to go into where the hopper is faulty. A couple of taps with her head in the right place and it's cow cake - her favorite. Number 143 tried to imitate her but she hadn't quite got the hang of it yet. A quick press of a button and all the girls got a treat of cake feed while being milked in the stalls. If you thought cows were dumb, then you were wrong. Number 64 even opens the doors by the handle if someone has forgotten to bolt it. She would have a wander around looking to see what mischief she could get up to!

The milk flowed through the glass tubes, along and down into the big glass collecting cylinders. It was creamy and thick. It then flowed along some more glass pipes and into two huge square stainless steel vats. I stretched up to peer inside through the viewing panel. The big paddles were swirling round and round like giant mixers. Natural milk and wholesome. Raymond, Geoff's brother, has been drinking it straight from the cow since he was a nipper and he is now in his mid-sixties. He's only a small chap but he can run rings around the young'uns and he is never ill. So there must be something in it!

After "Good mornings" to everyone, I reversed my truck up to the end barn, slid the huge double doors open and reversed in. I send clouds of dust up from the dry earth and even more dust when I applied the air brakes. I hitched up the 3 ½ ton trailer and Cat digger. I pulled out into the yard and got out of the truck. I had to choose my path very carefully, it was a bit like hopscotch. I had to avoid the cow pats as I didn't fancy smelling of cow pooh all the way to France.

Just one more job, I had to change a wheel on the trailer. There just hadn't been enough time beforehand.

Finally, with a sigh of relief, I was ready. I waved goodbye to everyone at the farm and returned to the flat, just a few minutes drive away. Yorkshire has some beautiful countryside and it's right on our doorstep. Unfortunately the towns and villages have been spoilt by bad planning, inconsiderate bad tempered people and binge drinking. The motorways have carved through it slicing south, west, east and north into chunks of busy noisy areas where it's hard to get away from the thundering trucks and high pitch whine of little cars flat out on suicide missions. You have to drive deep into the countryside to hope to get away from it all. Let's face it the UK is overcrowded.

# Sad farewell

Arriving back at the flat it was just turned 7am, any later and I wouldn't have been able to find a parking space. I gave Sue and our two Siamese cats a cuddle. I passed her a big parcel of drawings to post for me, the culmination of a lot of sleepless nights. One last check, had I got everything, was the fridge working as it was full of fresh food for my journey? Passport? Ticket? There was no way that I could miss Sue's suitcases. They were full and huge. Enough clothes for any eventuality, not to mention handbags and shoes. In her defense I had enough tools loaded on the truck to open a hire shop! I gave her a sloppy kiss and cuddle and said goodbye. Sue in turn wished me a Bon voyage!

I climbed into the truck and waved at the same time looking in the mirrors. Leaving her behind standing there, suddenly I was overcome with odd feelings. This was it! I would be driving to Southern France on my own for the first time. It was going to be a lonely fourteen hundred kilometers.

Making my way to the motorway just a few minutes away I noticed it was very busy, but then I remembered it was a bank holiday, something I had been trying to avoid. Oh well, best laid plans and all that.

Cutting across to the Great North Road I met a convoy of trucks heading south. They were tarted up in all their glory. Big chrome exhaust pipes, airbrushed murals on every panel and paintwork so highly polished it sparkled. I realised they must be on their way to a truck festival. I gave the lead truck a blast with my very loud air horn as I passed. I got the usual flash of lights to say I was clear to pull in.

The journey south was very uneventful. Except that by the time I passed Lincolnshire there were convoys of trucks heading north and that continued until I reached the M11. Presumably they were all heading for the same festival.

The miles melted away behind me. The sun was shining and it was getting warmer. Traffic was now at a standstill. The motorway was a huge car park as I neared the Dartford Crossing.

Sitting in the traffic gave me time to ponder. My thoughts were firmly fixed on my new adventure. I just couldn't wait to be free of all the hustle and bustle of England and to be settled in our little bit of France. It was still a dream but the dream was getting closer. Once passed Dartford it seemed no time at all before I was checking in at Dover.

As I weighed in at just over 10.5 tons and had gas on board I was sent to a special safety area. After checking it was safe I was on the ferry and on my way to France.

The helpful staff in the trucker's cafeteria suggested I stick with the chicken and chips. It was most certainly gluten free - yep! It was that and very boring too!

# French disco alfresco

Arriving in Calais I made my way to the truck park where I planned to fill up and stay the night. It was early evening, very sunny and hot and the new truck park was full. I just managed to get a space. I telephoned Sue to let her know I had arrived safely. I could tell by the tone in her voice that she was missing me and wished she had come with me in the truck. Now very tired, I set my bed up and drifted off to sleep in the cosy warm cab.

Boom, Boom, Boom. "What the bloody hell's going on?" Drifting in and out of my comatose state was I dreaming about music? No! "What time is it?" I was talking to myself again! It was 3 o'clock in the morning. I peered out from under my sleeping bag and looked towards where I thought the noise was coming from. Some bloody nutters were having a party in the car park. Boy racers, young girls screaming, giggling and dancing about like demented fools. I was in a confused tired state. Where was I? In the UK? No I was in France.

It was obvious I was not going to get any more sleep so I got up, had a wash to revive myself and decided to get an early start. It was quite warm compared to what it would have been at the same time back in Yorkshire. I turned the ignition key, something was wrong. The dash lights were dim and no power to the starter motor. In true Victor Meldrew style I shouted out, "I don't believe it."

I realised I had left the fridge on all evening and night and had drained one of the batteries. My heart sank. I had one of those flash back moments. I saw my big battery booster on the workshop shelf back in Barnsley. I had had to decide back then, large case of screws or 24 volt booster. I had thought I might make something when I got to Cayriech. Fool! I knew I should have brought it.

I unloaded the generator and small charger. I tried and tried but there was just not enough power to do the job. Think, think, think! Ah! Jump leads. No good as I wouldn't get anywhere near close enough. Ah! The digger battery and jump leads. It was worth a try. I found myself asking questions and answering myself out loud. Just one minor problem, the truck was 24 volts and my Cat digger was 12 volts. I had to decide which battery was flat.

"I am only going to get one go at starting the engine." I was now continually talking to myself. I had totally lost the plot. "Is there enough charge in the Cat battery?" If anyone was watching me they must have thought I was completely bonkers!

It was not an easy job getting to either of the batteries and the other problem was that I was trying to do things as quietly as possible. I didn't want to wake the other truckers, they might just put my lights out!

A very long 2 hours later, I was relieved to hear the engine start first time. Luckily I had packed the tools to do the job. Finally I was on my way south. I was now telling myself off for making so many mistakes and wondering what was going to happen next!

# Decisions decisions!

Eenie meenie miney mo! Which way shall I go? I heard myself saying. I was toying with Paris or Rouen in my head and out loud too as I approached the fork on the autoroute. I had to choose.

Isn't it great when there is no set time, no set route and no rush to get somewhere? Well two out of three ain't bad. As long as I got to our petite Moulin before Sue arrived at Toulouse airport I was onto a winner! I only had myself to worry about which cut out a lot of stuff that goes on between couples when travelling together.

You know the arguments.

"I said you should have stopped at that last restaurant to eat, everywhere will be closed by the time we find somewhere."
I knew you should have filled up at that last petrol station."
"I'm bursting for the loo, when's the next services?" "We've just passed it. "Why didn't you tell me we were passing the services?" And so on....!!

I took a right turn and headed for Rouen, the scenic route south, missing Paris on a Sunday might be a wise move. I had been stuck in traffic on the Peripherique before.
I wasn't a fan of that route anyway, I just thought I would have a leisurely drive and the scenery would take some of the boredom out of

driving alone. That was something you couldn't avoid on the autoroute down to Paris, although the ring road could be great fun!

Once on the Rouen road I suddenly hit a wall of dense fog covering my windscreen like a blanket. I slowed to a snail's place tentatively moving forward, winding down my window listening as if to compensate for my loss of sight. My nervousness told me to pull off the road but then the tip of a huge wind turbine blade cut through the fog and disappeared then re-appeared as if in slow motion. There was no sight of the support. It was a very strange sight as the blades just swooped out from the cloud.

The turbines reminded me of an old 60's horror film where a huge pendulum blade was swinging back and forth and moving slowly towards someone lying strapped on a table waiting to be sliced up. Yep! A bit bizarre. I had some French cheese for tea, had that got me dreaming?

There were several of them along the road and I was mesmerised for a time. Then I noticed a wide red mark caught in my headlights on the road up ahead and it headed towards the hard shoulder. As I got closer I realised something big must have been hit. It had obviously been dragged along and bits of car bumper were lying about the green and white dividing barrier was damaged and covered in blood. I'd better keep my eyes open as I didn't want to hit a wild deer or some other animal.

Another flashback moment popped into my head. Five years earlier when we were in Northern Germany buying our Hymer motorhome, we took a short cut across a rugged mountainous wooded area from the motel back to the dealer. Making our way up the winding fir-tree lined road there was a huge sign. Now, imagine looking out of your car windscreen which is cracked all over, and seeing a full size deer (cartoon drawing) with legs out stretched and it's face pushed against the screen looking in at you. Well that was the sign and it read: Achtung! Deerzeesplatteen!!! Made us laugh!

Back to the present. I dropped down a gear to climb a hill and I couldn't help noticing to my right there was a small deer trapped and running up and down between the motorway barrier and a fence. It's big brown eyes looked straight at me. It froze as I passed it slowly up the hill. It looked terrified. Perhaps it's mum was the road kill I had just passed. I hope it got away safely.

The roads were very quiet as expected so I had no delays and made good time. As I crossed the Seine at Rouen wispy morning mist was still rising off the river. It had a grey eerie look but it was calming at the same time. It's funny when you're driving alone your mind just wanders about. My mind was acting like a multimedia computer taking snapshots and short videos of life around me in vivid detail and colour. It's probably a bi-product of my dyslexia.

I make my family laugh when we're out anywhere as I constantly tell them, "Look at that or that." Things that would normally go unseen and they usually miss it and think I am pulling their legs. Some stuff goes to my subconscious for later retrieval. Sometimes another incident suddenly sends a pulse to my brain and a picture pops up! Perhaps I'll get committed one day!

The terrain is fairly flat and sparse on the way to Chartres as it is a big farming area. I passed through a village's narrow high street, dishevelled and forlorn, a victim from the constant barrage of thundering trucks day after day driving through.

As I approached Chartres I could not help but notice the magnificent cathedral spire towering above the town in the distance. Another place to mark on the map for a visit when we have more time. The early morning sun was trying to get through the cloud so I was able to take in the scenery along the way.

I had a little hold up when I came across a car boot sale in full swing. The organisers were slowing down what traffic there was. As I slowed to a crawl I got a good view between the two farm buildings where people were coming and going. There was some interesting antique furniture and pictures on sale. It looked like a quality place to visit. I received a friendly wave from a man an appreciative gesture for me driving slowly. During week days this was a main trunk route with huge trucks flying through, passing on the narrow road and missing each other by inches at times.

Snacking on the way, I decided to stop for some late breakfast. I found a quiet Aire with trees and wildlife and obviously a loo. One thing about France and travelling is that you are not denied good facilities. Well the toilets leave a lot to be desired at times. I got settled. I tried to put the kettle on ready for a nice cuppa but my inverter just wouldn't work, perhaps the flat battery I had had back in Calais was the cause. I couldn't be bothered to check out what the problem was or fit up the gas hob so I just had a cold drink instead with my crunchy nut cornflakes.

A couple of cars pulled in to use the loos and have a break from driving. I called out a cheerful bonjour. It was nice to talk to someone other than myself. Bonjour monsieur said the stranger giving me a funny look. Perhaps he thought I was a gypsy and who could blame him as I looked like a gypsy the way I was travelling.

With breakfast over I was soon on my way heading down to Orléans. I managed to take a wrong turn. It was one of those moments when you see a sign and I should have gone left but for some unexplained reason I went straight on. I knew I should have stopped and turned around but I carried on going. I wasn't lost, I just ended up having a nice drive through and around Orléans. More strange looks from people ensued as I drove the city centre. It was probably the British plates.

I was quickly back on track with familiar surroundings. I was missing the comments Sue and I would make to each other about houses being so close to the road, buildings we saw along the way, spotting wildlife and such like. Sue would often try to teach me some French. Yes, it can be lonely driving.

# Toxic smell had me running for the hills

There weren't many trucks on the road due to weekend driving restrictions, luckily they didn't apply to my truck. If I came across one I would set the cruise control to 90kph and sit behind it and see how far we kept together before I had to slow down or overtake. I travelled 30kms before the truck in front turned off. Then I had a jockey with another truck. First I overtook him, then he overtook me, then me again. Each of us would give a wave as we passed and then flashed our lights to say it was all clear to pull in. It was a bit of a buzz when a UK truck passed. He gave a blast on his horn and a flash of his lights. It gave me a happy feeling that I wasn't alone.

The sun had burned the haze away and the air was clear and fresh. You could see for miles, just a few grey clouds lingering on the distant horizon. I was so glad the weather seemed to be getting better as camping, tents and rain isn't a good mix. The wind farms had grown to tremendous numbers. What an array of turbines. I had never seen so many. I am glad I don't live in this area I hate constant wind.

I started having one of my scenario moments. I tend to conjure up scenarios at will. I imagined a poor Brit looking for a house in these parts and asking the agent, "What's the weather like around here does it get windy." "Oh, non Monsieur….just sign on the dotted line!"

I had to stop to refuel and have a welcome stretch from the monotonous driving position. I made a quick phone call to the owner of the gates I was carrying telling her I would see her tomorrow. I thought I would get a few more kilometres behind me before stopping for a very late lunch. Like I said I was snacking most of the way down due to boredom. It was a bloody good job I didn't do long distance driving for a living as I might well end up being 22 stone instead of just 10.

Buzzing along at a steady 90kph the roads were quiet so I put on the CD French Foundation Course by Michel Thomas to while away some time. It was just getting to the interesting bit where you learn how to say bonjour! "What's that smell?" I asked myself. I couldn't quite make it out. My sense of smell is pretty dire most of the time but it smelt like burning wire. I switched on the truck's computer to do a check for fault warnings. It gave the thumbs up symbol and said no warnings. I checked the mirrors for any smoke that might be coming out from somewhere. All clear.

It was getting stronger. It smelt familiar and very strong. I opened the windows to try and blow it out somehow but it was all outside and getting stronger by the minute. I started feeling sick. It was intoxicating. My eyes started to water and then the penny finally dropped. Before me, way up ahead, all I could see was field upon field of yellow flowers in full bloom. Not just a few fields but absolutely everywhere on both sides of the autoroute and as far as the eye could see. Just the odd green field dotted about. But everywhere else there were rape seed plants by the million.

The air was so thick I could hardly breathe. I was going to have to endure mile after mile of it. My head started to hurt. I felt I was being poisoned. I could not avoid it in any way. My headache was getting worse and I was feeling sicker as each mile passed. I tried not to breathe too deeply.

I was running out of driving hours but I just had to escape before I choked. I knew that as soon as I hit the Limousin region and climbed the hills I would be free. I battled on for what seemed like hours. Finally, I stopped at a very busy Aire just north of Limoges. I was relieved that I could take in some clean air again but my head was pounding through lack of food, rest and a cup of tea!

# Willies galore

There were several coaches in the parking area as I drove round to the truck park. I only just managed to find a space. I had to queue for the toilets where I could wash my face to rid myself of the pollen from the yellow peril. It was very busy. The smell of food and coffee bars as I passed through the services made me feel worse.

I had managed to find a parking space next to a central grassy area where people were sitting at tables resting and eating. The evening was very warm and pleasant. The French certainly know how to relax. I was a little envious when seeing couples sitting, eating and chatting. I was feeling a little lonely people watching. It's surprising how much information you can pick up just by observing.

I opened the side shutter on the truck and unloaded the food boxes. I fitted up my aluminium bench to use as a table, connected up the hob to the gas and put the kettle on. My 2kw inverter was playing up so I was lucky that I could use the gas instead. I took a couple of paracetamol as I was now feeling terrible. Talk about a watched pot never boils. I was gasping for a cuppa. Eventually gulping down 2 cups of hot tea one after the other and it was like nectar. I sat and rested for a while. My eyes were heavy and I thought I could still smell the rape seed, but I knew I was imagining it.

I needed to force myself to do things so I decided to have a fry-up. That would clear up the sickly feeling! I could, of course, have had a healthy salad as I had enough in the two fridges to last several days but that would not be the same! Finding all the kit in the truck was not a problem. The big walk-in box, although full to capacity, was shelved out and organised. I grabbed the frying pan, tossed in some bacon, a nice thick juicy 100% pork sausage, some mushrooms and an egg from the farm back in Barnsley. All was fried in butter! Not a healthy meal I know but I had endured an ordeal so it was my treat.

It smelt beautiful and my mouth was watering as I was cooking. I was sure people were licking their lips as they passed by because their pace certainly slowed for an inquisitive look.

I had just sat down on the bench in the truck park and was ready to get stuck in when, 2 coaches pulled up. They were parallel to me and the grass central area which contained a row of very low bushes. Everyone got off the coaches. They had obviously been drinking and they looked like a football or rugby team. They were big blokes. One guy in a suit was directing everyone and giving orders. He then rushed across to the service shop with a small group but about 20 of the blokes stood in line in full view of everyone sitting at tables, got their willies out and started to pee into the bushes and grass. So there they were about 20 willies pissing and some were quite proud of what they had in their hands and waved them about whilst singing some sort of rugby chant. They looked at each other with knowing smiles and laughter thrown in. The lady sitting in front of me eating a baguette sat motionless with the baguette poised in her mouth as she watched the spectacle. At the same time I took the full sausage that was on the end of my fork out of my mouth and slowly put it back in the frying pan. My mouth was still open. I suddenly realised what was happening, took a gulp of hot tea and almost choked. I thought about getting a video or photo because no one would have believed me. I had second thoughts as it would definitely look a bit pervy!

I've heard of rugby tackle but that lot took the biscuit!

It could only happen in France!!!

Shortly afterwards everyone piled back on to the coaches and they drove off. For the most part no-one had taken a blind bit of notice. Back in the UK there would have been road blocks and riot police. After the coaches left it started to quieten down as dusk descended. The services were full of trucks. They would have been there since Saturday lunchtime and were waiting to leave early Monday morning. I knew I wouldn't need to set an alarm clock as the roar of about 50 trucks leaving at around 5 am would soon wake me up.

I went into the services to get the key to the shower block which was reserved for truckers. God they were in need of refitting. I got a hot shower but I couldn't wait to get out. They certainly had a problem with ventilation and mould growth.

Back at the truck I fixed the screens around the windows to block out the service area lighting, climbed into my sleeping bag, I sent a text to Sue, good night and she text Bonne nuit back and in no time at all it was dreamland here I come. Zzzzzzzzzzzzzzzzz!

# The lonely road

As predictable as the rising sun, one by one the lorry drivers started their powerful engines, pausing waiting for the air pressure to build before they could engage a gear and release their brakes and off they drove, to the start of a new day.

It took almost an hour for the lorry park to clear. I lay awake thinking of all the far off places they might be going. I was no stranger to long distance driving. When we first got married I worked for an East London shop fitting firm delivering to all corners of the UK. Back then I was driving almost non-stop to Cornwall from London then spent the rest of the week making my way back via Bristol calling at shops. It was and still is a lonely job.

Climbing out of the truck it was still dark but glancing east I could see the light of the distant sun filtering through on the far horizon. It was slightly chilly so I decided, when in Rome, or as in this case it was France, do as the French do and I gingerly looked around before peeing at the side of the truck. It wasn't something I was used to and I felt awkward. The sloping tarmac caused a tiny river of steamy pee to head towards my shoes. I had to step back several times and was now a few feet away from the truck and in full view of anyone passing. I was unable to hurry, a combination of age, tea and a chilly morning, but finally I finished feeling like a naughty little boy. I couldn't climb back into the cab quick enough. I was feeling quite cold by now whereas my sleeping bag was still warm and inviting. I wriggled back in and tried to have an extra half hours sleep. It wasn't to be as I was restless and eager to get going.

Opening the roller shutter to the truck's rear workshop revealed a vast assortment of building tools. Some were on shelves and some were hanging on rows of hooks but crammed into every available space and almost to the roof, were boxes of food and camping gear. I should say glamping gear which seems to be the in-word. Not only did I have two portable fridges but there was a microwave, a sandwich maker, a portable oven, TV with Sky box, an 80cm satellite dish, a bread maker and not forgetting the cuddly toy. Luckily I had packed it all well otherwise I might have been attacked by tins of beans or the other heavy objects that were waiting to spring out like a jack-in-box on the journey from the UK.

I unloaded a few big plastic containers of food which enabled me to get to the large gas bottle and hob and most important the kettle. I set up my gas hob and got breakfast ready. That was all part of the trip and something to be enjoyed as there was no clock watching, no telephone ringing, no clients to see and no deadlines to meet.

Being Coeliac it's a lot easier to fend for myself rather than use the services and go through the seemingly long process of explaining my diet and checking ingredients. I had gluten free bread for my toast that I had baked before leaving the UK so it was home from home. I could have been stranded there for a week and survived quite easily with the amount of food and water I had on board. After breakfast I used the services for a wash, returned to the truck and did a safety check of the truck and trailer before continuing my journey south.

I realised it was Monday and the traffic had built up, mainly trucks. I say traffic, but nothing like what we see in the UK with all three lanes bumper to bumper on the M1 into Leeds or the mad ever decreasing circle of the M25. I got up to speed and slotted into the orderly line of trucks. I felt well rested and was now eager to reach my destination. Cayriech, the sanctuary, call it what you will, a piece of France that someday will be home.

I was constantly passing the large brown and white signs for all the various towns along the journey. They depict with images what the place is famed for. Some are renowned for their château, some for their churches and often the produce of the area. The names of the places are so, well, so French. Names like Châteauroux and La Souterraine. They conjure up all sorts of images in my head. The names and images make you want to visit and explore. I visualise tiny streets, medieval buildings, magnificent churches and pretty independent shops selling cheeses and wine.

I then thought back to some names of places in South Yorkshire, like Grimethorpe, Wombwell or Greasbrough. What a contrast. Someone must have had a sense of humour. Then there are the names I just love to say, like Saint-Cirq-Lapopie and Rocamadour. They just roll off the tongue. As well as so many names that I can't even imagine how to pronounce. One place we have to visit one day is Pierre Buffiere. The town clings to a hillside above a deep sharp valley with a river below. We have passed it so many times clearly visible from the autoroute south of Limoges. The viaduct crosses the river as it circles around the hill and the medieval town looks so inviting.

I stopped off at Brive to top up my bottomless fuel tank. It pays to know the areas where you can get fuel at the best prices. It was a tight squeeze at the pump that was built for cars but thankfully no one complained as I took up half the service station much to the bemusement of onlookers. Yes, I am in France where I find tolerance a whole lot nicer. Back in the UK I wasn't even allowed to stop for a minute at a supermarket. Now what was the reason? Oh yes, it was Health and Safety!! The UK can take EU regulations to a whole new level.

# Rendezvous

I phoned a French forum member from my mobile to say I would be with her in about an hour with the gates and big heavy posts. We arranged the rendezvous point at the first péage on the new autoroute.

The sun was rising fast. The intensity of the light never ceases to amaze me. It makes even the most dreary colours come to life. Everywhere the striking definition of vivid colours overloads my senses with pleasure, from the smallest wild flowers on the side of the road to the magnificent birds of prey with their plumage in varying tones of brown with dashes of cream. They are often seen sitting on fence posts along the journey. Their big eyes transfixed, watching, waiting and I catch their attention sometimes and their heads jerk in short movements following my gaze as I pass. I am in awe of these magnificent creatures.

The roads were now quieter as I got further south. I was able to look around and take in the beautiful landscape that constantly changed mile after mile.

It was a beautiful morning and I felt alive with enthusiasm. To be there driving south towards our little place instead of battling through the morning mad rush back in the UK. Normally it's a grey, gloomy time when you wish you were somewhere else. It then struck me. I WAS somewhere else. It made me glow inside and I felt so relaxed I could have stopped on the side of the road and gone walking and exploring the countryside without a care in the world.

No matter how many times I drive through this way I always feel that I am seeing the scenery for the first time. There's always something different to see. Everywhere looks clean and fresh. I watched out in case I spot birds of prey. Maybe I would get another glimpse of a wild deer in the lush green valley next to the autoroute with the little stream running through it. I never get tired of looking

I turned off the autoroute north of Souillac. Once I was through the péage and was approaching the roundabout I got a flash of lights from a van that was coming from my right. I acknowledged with a wave. That was good timing I thought.

I drove further on and stopped at a dusty limestone pull off point. I was greeted by a lovely young lady and her beautiful blonde haired, blue eyed baby daughter. She was sitting in her baby seat and securely strapped in. She certainly had her mother's looks. It is so nice to meet lovely people.

After a little chat I loaded the gates and posts into her van. I was presented with a bottle of wine, some homemade whisky marmalade and a generous gesture towards my fuel. I was going all cooey eyed and talking baby talk but she was not having any of it. This little outing had upset her routine and feeding time. I wish this lovely young lady, her French husband and family all the very best. They know who they are!

After goodbyes I made my way towards Souillac as there was no way back onto the autoroute. Driving down the long winding road, Souillac nestled in a deep valley along the banks of the river Dordogne. A great place to visit and for kayaking on the river. Although, I've yet to explore it. Just another place to add to a very long list.

The new autoroute that cuts through the landscape is something to be enjoyed. The toll road is normally quiet as the French don't like paying tolls. I was passing through valleys that you would not have seen had the road not been here. The white rock was dazzling in the sunlight but with hints of greenery that were slowly taking over the man-made scars. Parts of the valley had been cultivated so there was a patchwork quilt of different stages of growth with some deep, rich, reddish-brown straight furrowed soil.

The road was carefully cut and seemed to perch on the inside curve of the winding valley as it followed the natural terrain. As I looked across to the half circle as the road curved I got a great view of man's achievement in engineering skills. In places the road slowly climbed then dove deep into another valley to cross yet another river. A little further on it disappeared around the other side of the hill then climbed out of the valley, reaching a dizzy height, before being swallowed by a huge five lane tunnel. Finally it emerged through the other side.

I am never disappointed with the vista. A wide screen panoramic picture as far as the eye can see. There were hills to the far left and right while the centre was lush cultivated land on a flat basin. Picture postcard houses with their shallow terracotta pitched roofs were dotted about here and there. Far away I could see a church spire and a pigeonnier, a white limestone viaduct that carried the rail line to Caussade standing tall above the canopy of trees, If you had the time to stop you could almost see the Pyrenees from this height

It had been raining, that fresh earthy smell seeped in through my open window. A few grey clouds hovered overhead but the temperature had been rising fast since I left the UK. The heat was evaporating the moisture which was clinging to my skin. I turned on the cab's fan and it brought in all sorts of aromas from the farms either side of the autoroute. Now down in the valley the road was straight and flat as I neared the exit for Caussade. I started to get butterflies. What changes could I expect? Who would be at the campsite? Would the Moulin be ok? So many unanswered questions. My head was filling with images of how things were when we left our little bit of France last year.

# Almost there

After paying the charges at the péage, I engaged first gear and roared off towards Cayriech. I had to suppress my apprehension as it seemed to quicken my pace. I had better not forget the 3 ton digger I was dragging behind on the trailer.

As I passed my local builders merchant on the outskirts of Caussade I gave them a blast of my deafening air horn, but "personne est la" ( nobody there ). They must have heard me coming and hidden in the sheds. I swept around the small ring road and the couple of roundabouts getting several stares from other motorists and passers by. Not much had changed. But for a little rain the day was perfect. I slowed to crawl over the speed bumps opposite the little school in Monteils. It was only a short hop now along the smooth quiet road that would be welcomed by any cyclist from the Tour de France. Tall picturesque plane trees lined the road. They are so common to these parts and give shade on the hottest of days.

The last few kilometers of my journey took me along a very familiar road with gently banked curves and bends. Little rustic farms and pretty houses along the way huddled amongst the greenery. The road climbed continually, eventually levelling out to reveal the valley to my left that I had just driven through. The autoroute was hidden below an engineered escarpment thus giving unbroken views across the carefully tended farmland. Little white stone farm buildings with terracotta tiled roofs stood proud above the lush green countryside. Everywhere had that Mediterranean feel about it and oozing calm and tranquility.

As I approached the last house on the left, before turning right, I saw there had been a change! Le Tourniquet was no more. The painted sign on a mill stone at the front gate was now blank. It no longer bore the name Le Tourniquet that had given me a smile for several years. No more imagining why it was called that. Perhaps they had paid their mortgage off. Perhaps the owners had sold it. One day I should call at the house and find out - or should I just keep imagining?

I made my way around the last long right hand bend before turning right towards the village of Cayriech. I felt my heart pounding in my chest. The strangest feelings and thoughts passed through me. Peering across the fields I saw the cattle were out feeding. It was a dairy herd of Holsteins, the same cattle that my friend back in the UK farms and breeds. It's a breed noted for milk production and calf bearing qualities. But they must be cared for as they carry a lot of weight and are prone to rear leg problems. Surprising what information you pick up. There's always something new to learn every day.

The narrow road twists and turns before dropping down to the village. I passed the large wooden cross at the junction. The village roof tops and church were now visible through the tree lined road. I had to pull over to let a car pass and I get a wave and a smile. I reached the sign announcing Cayriech, proudly displayed and surrounded by beautiful flowers. Another sign below it states that the village is famed for its flora and forna.

I slowly made my way over the little hump-back bridge that's only wide enough for one vehicle to pass. I stopped and peered into the river below. The crystal clear, sparking water flowing underneath was a wonderful sight. A small shoal of fish darted away from the sound and vibration of my truck and headed downstream to disappear under some floating weed swaying in the current.

The beautifully kept village was living up to its reputation. Strange to think that back in the UK we have visited "best kept" villages and thought how nice it would be to live there and here we were about to live in one but in France. Who would have imagined it seven years ago when we were sitting in a village pub in Yorkshire talking about this very thing over a meal with our best friends. Sadly Dick had cancer and was no longer with us which in a strange way guided us to Cayriech.

Turning right out of the village and barely getting into second gear I gazed across to the park. Open to all. With carefully tended flower beds in full bloom and an ancient large rustic stone table with freshly planted flowers in pots on top. A jackdaw swooped passed followed by a magpie. Wildlife in abundance.

## Surprises all around

I took a wide right hand turn into the campsite. As I stopped the air brakes, the air relief valve give a loud shuuush sound and created a plume of dust from the limestone drive. It rose up all around and then floated off. I looked across to the overnight camping area. What a surprise. Peter, Eileen, Bob and Joan were walking down to greet me. Peter was hobbling along with a walking stick. He had had a cycling accident in Spain. Peter, a keen cyclist, had collided with a Belgian on an outing. He ended up having a new hip replacement and was still in some pain.

They had arrived in Cayriech early from Spain in convoy. Bob was helping Peter with the journey. They were on the way back to the UK and had anticipated my arrival. They looked somewhat puzzled. I had failed to mention that Sue would be flying over to Toulouse from Manchester. Almost immediately I was greeted by Remy and Jocelyne my friends and campsite owners. They were very pleased to see me but also very puzzled too. Where was Susan they asked. I explained in my best French that she was following over by airport. Yes, I know! I am still learning French of course I meant avian and not aéroport
French kissing, hearty handshakes and big smiles all round then general chit chat. It was good to be there. It felt more like home every second.
It started to drizzle while I unhitched the trailer and digger. Remy suggested that if the rain got heavier I should stay in the house for the night rather than try and put the tent up. The generosity and friendship

warmed my heart. But I was determined to beat the rain and so I parked the lorry next to one of the pitches. The rain was now falling heavier as I walked back to Peter's motorhome for a catch up chat and a cuppa.

## Glamping in Cayriech

It wasn't long before the rain stopped and the sun was fighting its way through. That was a relief. I didn't want Sue arriving to bad weather. I made my way back to the tent pitch. Peter and Bob followed to give me a hand, then Remy arrived, then the chap from the next pitched came over, then my friend who distributes the local free papers arrived. Before long I had a small crowd of helping hands.

I unloaded and unpacked the tent. Back in the UK Sue and I had watched the video and got the tee shirt of how to erect our new tent. But this was the first time it had actually been out of the bag!

With all the helping hands we painstakingly connected and threaded the poles through the tent. They were all following my instructions until we got to the last of the front poles. Something is wrong!

Those poles should not have been here. They should have holes in them. Bugger! We pulled out all the poles but none had holes. Nothing else for it so I set up the laptop, propped it on the back of the lorry and inserted the instruction CD. There we were, six blokes, gathered around a laptop discussing how to do it, in French and English, rewinding time and again looking for some sign of the poles with holes. We were all scratching our heads.

One thing I have come to realise in France is that if a job has to be done there will always be a small gathering of people discussing how to do something and how not to do something. There will be lots of gesticulating, shrugging, raising of eyebrows and pointing. I just truly love it!

We finally came to a joint Anglo-French conclusion that the instructions were for an older model and this newer one did not have holes but had clips. Clever these little slanty eyed eastern yellow people. They know how to play us. I could just see them back at the factory in Shenzhen laughing and making fun. "Ah, so, packed wrong instructions for the UK, velly clever!"

Anyway, all ten of us now had a bit of tent each. Yes, I know the crowd just got bigger. I couldn't leave the Dutch or Belgians out now could I?

We walked the tent forward as per instructions and hey presto it was up. Simples! "Le château for the kings!" Remy exclaimed. The nine man Vango tent was big enough to swing a giraffe in let alone a cat. Sue had wanted space and we certainly had space! We also blocked out the sun for several other pitches!

Congratulations all around. Pleased smiling faces of the helpers and on-lookers. Were they expecting a family the size of a football team to arrive to take up residency? No, just the two of us I told them. They jokingly asked about satellite TV. "Oui," I said and smiled. "They call it glamping back in the UK." That was a remark that left me with a challenge. Arm waving and "sounds like" abound but I got there in the end. After more smiles and plenty of "bon courage" the small crowd dispersed to let me get on with unloading the truck.

The mammoth task of unloading the truck and getting set up took me into darkness and hence a distinct lack of food. It was then that Peter turned up to invite me up to their motorhome where Eileen had prepared a lovely hot meal. It was just like old times except that Sue was still in the UK. After a pleasant relaxing evening I returned to my tent and collapsed into a deep sleep on my new camp bed.

Waking up in complete darkness and silence it took me a few moments to work out where I was. Very disorientated I staggered around until I found a torch. Very odd feelings overcame me I was on my own.

Sue was, of course, back in the UK. We have hardly ever been apart for very long in the last 38 years. Yes, I'm a big softie.

A visit to the loo was required - it's an age thing and finally I returned to my camp bed and drifted off again.

The early morning light stirred me from my slumber and looking skywards the flickering sunlight through the trees was casting animated shadows on the tent. Birds were singing in the trees above and further away they were calling to each other. Footsteps crunched on the white limestone gravel path outside. There were distant voices and gentle civilised sounds. I lay there thinking that just a few days ago back in the UK the sounds were very different. Cars, scooters and trucks dashing about, parents shouting at their children to hurry up or be late for school, a small dog yapping tethered to a post outside a shop, an ambulance racing past with its siren echoing and bouncing off the buildings, then another as it left the depot just up the road from our flat in Barnsley. There must be another accident on the motorway nearby. The sounds carried on throughout the day in an endless rushing about always creating an anxious stressful environment. Have I awoken in heaven?

It was a very sluggish start to the day. I didn't have to pick Sue up from the airport until two in the afternoon. I could take my time over a relaxing breakfast of cereal followed by toast with big dollops of marmalade and several cups of tea. I resisted the urge to go to the mill. I had plenty to do as I had to get the tent ship shape for Sue's arrival.

The weather had improved dramatically. I wasn't surprised as this area has its own micro climate and can be quite predictable. The temperature was rising and the sun was climbing high in the sky. Steam was rising off the damp grass and the gravel paths as the sun's heat intensified. I was feeling very relaxed.

During the meal the previous evening Peter and Eileen had suggested that I use their car to pick Sue up from Toulouse Airport. An offer I couldn't refuse.

# Together again!

The airport was just a forty minute hop on the autoroute from Caussade. I arrived with plenty of time to spare so I was able to park right outside the arrivals area. I sat waiting in the hot afternoon sun, watching the comings and goings. There were the obvious signs of expats waiting for friends and relatives whilst other Brits were holding up cards for Mr & Mrs Smith or somebody or other.

I got so engrossed in my people watching that I only just noticed Sue at the last minute. She had clothes on that I had not seen before. Silly me! "I have had this dress for ages but I just had to find some shoes and hand bag to match. You've seen it before," said Sue. I scratched my head,........nothing changes!

I took her hand and looked into her eyes as the bright sunlight lit up her face, my heart melted as I saw that same little girl look I saw when we had a chance meeting in a doorway in Devon in the summer of 1972. Her big eyes and smile gets me every time! It was lovely to be together again. France isn't the same without her. She was tired, having been up since 4am travelling over the Pennines to Manchester Airport and was glad to have her feet firmly on the ground. As I led her to Peter's car, she was a little surprised but pleased with our mode of transport back to Cayriech.

We arrived back to welcoming hugs and kisses from Peter, Eileen, Remy and Jocelyne. After long conversations about everything and anything we all went our separate ways and turned in for an early night.

We both had a good sleep in the new single camp beds which were very comfortable. Sue was wrapped up in a double duvet and was snug as a bug. As usual I was first up. The light just triggers my senses so I just have to get up. It drives Sue mad. I could hear her complaining about the noise I was making getting breakfast and well, just breathing! She wanted a lay in. For those that haven't been camping it's almost impossible to be quiet in a tent.

A lazy morning in the hot sun took us up to lunchtime. I set the table up, then the four wooden chairs and searched for the canvas seats and backs. Oh no! I had left them back in the UK.

"That's bright." Sue exclaims, "What else have you forgotten?"

"I won't know until I can't find it," I reply. Fortunately we had bought a couple of new chairs when we got the tent. So all is not lost.

After lunch, Peter, Eileen, Bob and Joan joined us for a walk down to the mill. It was the first time Bob and Joan had been and they were looking forward to seeing just what we had bought.

We expected to see a bit of a jungle but we weren't prepared for the seven foot high wall of vegetation that confronted us. It ran from our fence right to the river. I know our land is fertile but this was going too far! There were new trees sprouting up everywhere. The weeds were a bit thinner between the mill and our grange. I opened our wire gate and trod a path to the river half expecting to see some lost tribe or wild animal.

The abundance of insects buzzing around kept us busy whilst trying to avoid the nettles. Finally we made it to the river. It was a lovely sight with the calm tranquility of the crystal clear water as it flowed over the waterfalls and glistened in the bright sunlight.

We walked along the river bank up to the top weir above our canal and gazed up-river. Large lily pads cloaked the still water and every now and again small ripples formed where fish were catching insects. The river is shrouded by a canopy of trees on both banks and they meet high up and form a tunnel effect. Narrow beams of sunlight shone through the trees forming light green patches on the river.

It was so peaceful except for the gentle sound of water trickling over the small ancient stone lock gates, the noise of birds and insects and all surrounded by the sound of a slight breeze in the trees. Any stress we may have been feeling just melted away.

We returned to the campsite with many exuberant greetings from the neighbours in the village. We understood completely why Remy called Cayriech paradise. People had time to talk and they seemed contented and happy with their life here.

The next few days were spent relaxing and chatting to fellow French campers that we had met before. Peter, Eileen, Bob and Joan were getting ready to leave for Lancashire. They had been away all winter and were looking forward to seeing their families. Besides, Peter had to report to Hospital for a check up.

We wished them a bon voyage and made plans to visit them when we returned to the UK. Eileen as usual had a tearful departure. Bob, a retired builder said he wanted to come and stay with us to help with our building work. Another offer we couldn't refuse!

# Busman's holiday

I had been itching to get started on the foundations of the Moulin. I had lounged about doing nothing but recuperating from the journey down for long enough. Monday was going to be the day to start work, proper. We had a very lazy Sunday morning watching the day go by and we went walking through the village, looking at the restored medieval buildings, once again being greeted by villagers. We felt we were outsiders but felt at home at the same time,

There is one unrestored house we just love. It has so much character. Plaster and paint peeling off, all of varying colours, the old steep rickety staircase exposed at the front leading up to the centre of the house, shutters and windows that must have seen so much life before and during the Nazi occupation, the oak colombage construction standing the test of time, plant pots filled with flowers, old cart wheels, the odd chair and other bric-a-brac lying around, all giving that time forgotten look. We know the owner so we will have to find out its history one day.

Despite the hot afternoon sun we decided to have a bike ride along the river. It was a gentle ride on the east bank. We passed the odd empty house, a couple of old farms - the occupants were even older - the moulin below ours, still under construction but looking good. We peered into the river and spotted shoals of fish. We got excited when we spotted an enormous carp cruising past. There was an old man sitting on the bank fishing for tiny fish that he put into an old white plastic paint tub. "Saving them for supper," he said.

We introduced ourselves. "Ah!" he exclaims, "Monsieur Colin, moulin, bon courage." He knew the previous owner. "A very important man," he said with some authority. With a handshake and an Au revoir we cycled on and eventually reached a small bridge over to the west bank.

We stopped on the bridge and peered into the waters below. There were trout of all sizes swimming into the current and then slipping into little eddies near the bank for a rest. Some darted below the bridge to escape into the darkness as they sensed our presence. They hid between the swaying weeds below the surface. I never tire of the local wildlife as it's so relaxing. We reflected on just how fortunate we were to be here but never losing sight of the less fortunate that we knew back in the UK.

Cycling on we passed a small plantation of trees all perfectly in line, diagonally and across. The tall straight trunks were meticulously tended. We turned right onto a perfectly straight road that led back to the village. One old farm building along this road was especially important to us. The collection of ramshackle outbuildings built from weathered ship lap and old stone housed a small timber mill. There was the ancient huge saw blade for cutting large trees along with even more ancient rollers that the huge trunks can roll along. There were rusty tools of all descriptions hanging on bits of scruffy string. Old cans, bits of metal, piles of sawdust on ledges, several small stacks of assorted timber lying about and tack hanging up for pulling logs. A little black horse greeted us with a loud neigh. We got off our cycles as she trotted over to us for a stroke. A very friendly little horse. We gave her a good scratch. She looked like she needed a good grooming. Talking to her gently we said goodbye.

We have some very large ash trees drying which will need cutting for furniture making. Another reason why this area is so special.

We reached the crossroads, turned right and crossed the little hump back bridge with the planters full of flowers - a welcoming sight for visiting tourists. Cayriech was put on the map by Madam Mulpas, the previous Mayoress who instigated the renovation of the entire village in the early nineties.

Eventually we arrived back at the campsite. We had our evening meal outside in the warm glow of the setting sun with the crickets chirping away. A passing camper wished us bon appetit. A perfect end to a perfect day. We went to bed and slept soundly in our mosquito free bedrooms.

We woke up to the wonderful sounds of nature. It was the opposite to the normal waking process we have back in the UK. There was no need for urgency, no beating the traffic build-up and the school run blockage. None of that. A steady start to a new type of working day. Possibly a French way or maybe just how we perceived it.

After a relaxing breakfast and shower I made my way to the parking area. I hitched the trailer up to the truck and drove the short distance to the Moulin. What wonderful surroundings to work in I thought. Sue soon arrived on her bike to help clear the vegetation and piled it up ready for burning.

I unloaded the digger and moved it to the back of the mill. I had to clear the stone that was left from last year when we demolished the gable end. We both worked hard and fast preparing the area for felling some trees and digging the new foundations.

The temperature soon got to us. We sat on some large stone steps that we had demolished and took refuge in the shade of the grange. Lunch time was upon us so we returned back to the tent, Sue cycled off while I followed on foot.

Un-restored house in Cayriech

## Grrrrr! She wont bite!

After a fresh crispy salad lunch and a good rest I left to go and do some more noisy work with the digger. Sue, on the other hand, had decided to go for a bike ride. I cycled down to the mill waving and calling out cheerfully to the gardeners and the odd-job men working at one of the village gites. I turned left up the track leading to the mill. As I did so, in the distance, I saw two figures walking towards me and coming from the direction of our mill. I stopped dead in my tracks. My heart was thumping away in my chest with fear! Also walking towards me was a dog. A big dog. A big Rottweiler dog. What should I do?

Thinking fast, mostly out of fear, I got off my bike and kept my bike between me and this very big dog. Then a voice called out, "Captain, I presume." I was more than a bit taken aback. "Hello, I am Neville and this is Louise my wife. Oh and this is Lottie. She doesn't bite! Come here Lottie…good girl."

It transpired that they were neighbours from just over the hill. They had read about us on one of the Internet French forums and had come to visit as they were over from the UK staying in their holiday home. I asked them to wait until Sue arrived. It was going to be a non-working afternoon.

When you have visitors you just have to have a good old chin wag. That was one of the reasons we were here to make time and take time for people and life. During our conversations I plucked up the courage to stroke Lottie. She looked at me through the whites of her eyes. I put on a brave face but inside I was trembling with fear.

The day seemed to, well, just roll along. We lost track of time and even what day it was. Such a great feeling. I can imagine it might be like that when people retire. No need for any urgency or time keeping. That's something I am looking forward to and soon I hope!

We had to go to Caussade to check the prices of concrete and arrange a delivery date.

As we drove over the village bridge in the truck we stopped to say hello to Neville and Louise who were out walking with Lottie. We got talking and continued our previous conversation. During our chat at the mill we had spoken about how they were thinking of extending their house. In passing I had mentioned that if they would like to trade favours I could do a drawing of what they wanted and they could show it to the new Mayor of Cayriech and in return Neville could cut down our vegetation with his new mammoth brush cutter that he had told us about. We said our goodbyes and thought nothing more of it.

At the builders merchant we were not surprised at the prices. They were more expensive than the UK. A full load of 7.5 cubic metres of concrete, with a delivery charge of over a €100.00, pushed the price up to €900.00. Saving the labour and time of mixing it ourselves it was worth it and we would be able to pour almost all the extended foundations in one go. So we placed an order and arranged to telephone the day before we needed it.

Yet another day in which nothing could be done. Shopping and sorting things out just eats into a day and especially when most places close for 2 hours at lunch time. It was one of the things we would eventually get tuned into. A very civilised way of life, Je pense!

We settled down for a lazy evening. Remy popped by to see how our visit to Caussade had gone. He gesticulated vigorously and replied, "très cher" (very expensive) when we told him the price of the concrete. He also asked why we needed so much. I explained that it was a big foundation. "Ah," he muttered with a puzzled face. With a bonne nuit he headed back to his house leaving us to get an early night.

Although I am an early riser, there still wasn't enough time to fit everything in. Little jobs like taking the rubbish and re-cycling to the bins, getting a shower, setting my bread maker going for my gluten free bread ate into the morning. At last we both made tracks to the mill. As we approached we saw that someone had beaten us to it. Much to our surprise Neville and Louise were there. Neville was wearing a blue boiler suit and was unloading his big, and very expensive, four wheeled brush cutter from his trailer. My throw away comment about trading some tasks a few days ago had been taken literally. He had come to tackle our huge jungle - all three acres of it.

We were amazed at the speed with which the cutter tore through it. It was very hot and the sweat was pouring out from under Neville's floppy bush hat. Up and down our fields he went with relentless stamina. He was working from the outside in making diminishing sections. As he got close to the end he spotted a snake but it was too quick for us to see and it disappeared into the deep undergrowth that lines our canal.

When he had finished I felt a little embarrassed. He had worked so hard and we had known them for only a matter of a week. It was truly humbling. We made plans to visit their house and measure up so I could draw up a proposal to show the mayor.

Neville and Louise's house was just over the hill from our place. It has very impressive stonework and is a sort of upside-down farmhouse that had been restored. The living area was on the first floor with bedrooms below on the ground floor. There was also a lovely barn and garage and all set on a nice elevated plot.

As we approached their gate Lottie bounded over to us barking. I was apprehensive of going in. Neville called her back to the barn entrance where it was perfectly shaded from the hot sun. Louise was seated at a small table and invited us to sit down. Lottie laid under the table and I was sat on a very low camping chair.

As we sat talking the subject came up as to why I was a bit uneasy with Lottie. "She doesn't like your hat," Neville said. Just then Lottie stood up in front of me and yawned in my face. I swear I could have fitted my head in her mouth like a performing lion tamer. Her huge, sharp, white pointed teeth could have finished me off with one gulp. I felt sure that I heard someone cry for help from the depths of her throat. Perhaps it was all in my mind. I sat there and froze. She looked at me, gave a little grrrrr, probably thinking it was too hot to bother eating me now and wandered off - thankfully.

Neville and I measured up the whole plot and buildings. I kept a watchful eye on Lottie's whereabouts. I didn't want her creeping up on me while I was taking photos of the house elevations that I could then draw up in an animated new design of the proposed extension. Luckily I had brought my laptop with me although my CAD computer was back in the UK. I would still able to do a nice design albeit a bit slower.

After tea it was time to return back to our tent. At the campsite, sitting quietly, we reflected on the lovely day we had had meeting some nice neighbours, the jungle was flattened so we could see the whole plot once again and discovering the trees that had self set in various places. We were also thinking how nice it would have been to have been able to afford a house that was finished and ready for living in. Our thoughts turned to dreams as we drifted off to sleep.

# Timberrrrrr!

We awoke to another warm sunny morning. I think we were getting spoilt. We had to fell a couple of trees, and as the truck was already at the mill we cycled down and worked out a plan of action.

It was obvious that I would have to climb the tree in front of the mill and cut off some big limbs first. The huge tree would cause a lot of damage if it were to fall onto the small bridge as all the weight was leaning the wrong way. The tree, a large ash, had grown to about forty foot. I put the ladder against it and went up with chain saw in hand. I felt a bit uneasy because if something went wrong I could fall and might well hurt myself! Nothing for it, I would have to buy a harness and I remembered seeing one in the hire shop in Montauban. We set off in the truck to get one.

The price of the safety harness, buying or hiring, was very high compared to the UK. Beside that the lanyard that was attached was short being for scaffold use and no good for trees. Thinking caps, on we drove to the Decathlon Sports hyperstore further on. The very helpful staff, and a young customer who was a climber, took great delight in sorting me out with some climbing gear. A hundred foot of bright pink rope, several attachments and a harness. Then I was given lessons on how to work them. One comment that rang warning bells in my ears came from the young French climber and it was along the lines of "Don't do this with that or you're MORT." A word that spoke for itself!

Back at the mill I eagerly got the harness set up and with rope attached I climbed up the tree and attached myself. If I was to fall I would not go far. I might have ended up upside down but I would not have gone to ground. Sue looked on from a safe distance whilst calling out to be careful as she didn't want to be arranging a box for me. Her confidence gave me all the support I needed!

First I tied off the huge limb that almost touched the front of the mill. I did an undercut of the branch with my chain saw, then I stood above it and braced myself as I cut the top, the huge limb parted company from the trunk, the tree swayed violently due to the weight that had been taken off. But I was safe! The precautions had paid off. I started to sing the Monty Python Lumberjack song to the smiling face of Susan!

Cutting the rest of the tree and dropping the huge trunk was a piece of cake. I then used the digger to drag it off to the barn to dry out for later use. Sue started separating the useful pieces of wood and piling the rest up for burning. Trimming off all the small branches with her bow saw and anvil croppers. It had been a long day with only a short lunch break so we deserved a much needed rest and after a hearty meal retired to bed.

My new found occupation had me up early. Sue was still tucked up in bed and was reluctant to get up. But today was the day for the big boy. Seventy five foot of mammoth tree that was only six foot from the mill. We had several high ones, some that were up to a hundred foot tall and they needed to come down as they were too close for comfort. They had been left to grow out of control. I had removed trees in the UK as part of building works but never on such a scale as this.

Once at the mill I propped my thirty foot ladder against the tree. Sue had just arrived and said, "Be careful" - slightly understating the obvious! Harnessed up and chainsaw in tow I climbed to almost fifty foot. The top limbs were still towering above me. Bits of tree were coming away in my hand as I ascended. At the bottom of the trunk there were signs that the tree was dying so I was climbing cautiously. I tied off at every safe point. I then stopped. I looked up, I looked down, I looked around and then said out loud, "What the bloody hell am I doing up here?" It was going to be a very difficult job. I decided to go back down, much to the relief of Sue who was standing at the bottom covering her eyes. Another plan of action was needed. Preferably one that didn't require me swinging around like Tarzan.

The towering tree had to fall between an awkward angled fifteen foot gap, between other trees and partly on to our neighbours field. I set about cutting out a wedge. My big bladed Sthil saw soon got through. I cut the back side and wedged it. It should fall now I thought, but it didn't. I cut some more, and then some more. It would not go! There was only a centre section of 10cm square left but that tree refused to budge. It was just balancing there.

I waited to see if the wind would blow it down but the air was still and hot. It simply would not fall. Bugger! There was nothing for it, I had to climb it again. I packed out the cuts with wedges and as I went up I prayed that it wouldn't decide to fall with me hanging on like some tree hugging nutter.

I attached a thick long rope three quarters of the way up. Then I got down in double quick time. With a watchful eye on the tree, I drove the digger in to the next field then scrambled through the undergrowth to retrieve the rope. Grabbing the rope I attached it to one of the securing points on the digger. I was only too aware that the tree weighed considerably more than my three ton digger. If it were to fall the wrong way then the digger, with me in it, could be pulled in any direction and with some force!

With complete confidence I set the diggers lever to full throttle, pulled back on the travelling controls, took up the slack and went for broke! The huge tree came crashing down towards me. From the safety of the cab I gave a shout of "Timberrrrrrrrr!" It landed exactly where I had planned for it to fall. "I think I deserve a Blue Peter badge for that," I shouted to Sue. She was standing far away up the track, looking relieved and pleased.

The task of cutting all the branches off and sectioning the trunk to be dragged off with the digger took us in to the following day.

The next day Sue and I cleared the immediate area around the mill. I could then start to mark out the ground ready for excavating the new foundations. It was a bit tricky to get the lines right as the old mill was out of square. The stone walls had lent over time and the dam wall had bulged but I got there in the end. The job was made easy with spray line paint, in a nice shade of fluorescent pink as that was all I could get from the builders' merchant. Silly me - I had left two full tins of white back in the UK.

It was time for lunch so I strolled back to the campsite. As soon as I arrived there Sue gave me some great news. Our eldest son Nathan and his girlfriend Lucy hoped to visit for a weekend if they could get a flight at a good price.

Neville and Louise were returning back to work in the UK so they invited us up to their house for chat before leaving. Thankfully I had finished the animated drawing of their house and extension. It looked very impressive with plenty of detail. It had been quite a long process working on it in the tent with only the laptop.

Lottie still had an evil eye on me, although I did stroke her and speak doggy talk to her. "Oh, Lottie you're a lovely girl. You're just a big baby." She looked at me from the corner of her eye and I felt sure she was thinking, "Who you trying to kid, I know I've got you quaking in your boots!"

I uploaded the drawing to their laptop and demonstrated the features. They both liked it. I hoped the mayor would too.

# Family arriving

The following day we decided to have a day off and do some shopping as our son was soon to arrive. When we got back, I set up the spare tent. Our pitch was big enough to take two large tents and I was now an old hand at putting up tents! Remy called by and exclaimed, "Extension for the château?" We had a good laugh and I explained that we expected Nathan any time soon.

Just then Neville and Louise called by to say that the mayor had liked the design and could see no problems with permission for a building permit. We were glad that the effort had paid off. We wished them a bon voyage as they were starting out on the long journey back to blighty the next morning.

The weekend was nearing and Nathan and Lucy were due on Friday afternoon at Toulouse airport. I readied the truck. It was a beautiful hot sunny day. I was so glad as I hadn't wanted them to arrive to bad weather. Sue had to stay in Cayriech as the truck only had two passenger seats.

The forty minute drive to the airport on the autoroute was a breeze. No sooner had I reached the arrivals pickup point they came walking towards me. They were both in colourful summer clothes and it was very a strange feeling as I felt that France was my home and my family were visiting us. After big hugs we got on our way.

During the journey back to Cayriech I just had to explain to them both not to expect too much. We hadn't got that far with the building work and it was merely a plot of land with a pile of stones. I suppose I was playing things down a bit. It all sounds a bit grand when you say you have a place in the south of France. We had been lucky when we found it, or perhaps it had found us.

As we arrived at Cayriech Sue was waiting with open arms. There were the usual hugs and kisses. Nathan may now be in his thirties but they are never too old for affection, even from Dads!

Remy popped in to say hello. I felt a little awkward knowing that Remy's son, in his twenties, had died a couple of years ago. Perhaps it was just my sensitive side but I am sure I could see sadness in Remy's eyes. All the same I had strange thoughts and feelings.

Sue had prepared a fresh salad lunch for us. It was lovely all sitting together in the hot sun, birds singing, other campers passing and a shouting a cheery bonjour and a departing bon appétit! All very civilised. We sat and relaxed whilst getting the low-down of all the happenings back in Yorkshire. A lot can happen in a few weeks.

I was itching to get to the mill. I nudged Nathan. "Are you ready for a walk?" I asked. They were a little surprised as they hadn't realised it was so close. They were expecting to drive to the mill. It was a very pleasant stroll through the village, greeting the gardeners who were busy keeping up the tradition of the best kept village and introducing my son to them was a proud Dad moment!

Nathan is a time served tradesman covering bricklaying, plastering and joinery who can turn his hand to anything. Takes after his Dad! Well someone's got to blow my trumpet. On the other hand, he also takes after Sue with his attention to fine detail and design, the use of colours and so on. It was important for me to get his take on the task ahead of us. Yes it is a big project but we are seasoned builders and designers having spent more than thirty years designing and building retail shops, flats and homes for clients - but when I started I was thirty plus years younger. As Nathan looked over the site I could see the cogs turning, taking it all in and suddenly he said, "There's a lot to do you will need some help." He wasn't wrong there.

We spent a good hour walking around our land. They just loved the river, the tranquillity and were surprised at just how much space we had.

We walked back through the village via a small back street. Yet again we were constantly greeting locals as we passed by. When we got back to the campsite a noisy family had turned up for the weekend in one of the cabins. They seemed fairly intent on getting drunk very early. We noticed that Remy was keeping an eye on them from afar. We were possibly in for a disturbed night.

We decided to have a nice relaxing evening so we ordered food from the campsite. A large bowl of fries, huge Toulouse sausages & haricots verts. Sue rustled up some fresh salad and we washed it all down with local chilled Monteils wine. The air was still and crickets were chirping away, the evening had that Mediterranean Atmosphere. The sun slowly set and the smell of barbeques filled the air. Bon appétit rang out as anyone passed by. Nathan and Lucy commented on how friendly everyone was. Another bottle of wine helped us sleep through any noise.

As usual I was up with the larks. Sue turned over. I could faintly see her through the wall of our adjoining compartment. Her camp bed creaked. It was slightly chilly. As I emerged from the tent I looked skyward and called out to Nathan and Lucy. "It's a lovely morning. Get up before you miss it!" "Go away, we're still tired," came the reply. I glanced across to the adjacent cabin. Something must have happened in the night as the terrace balustrade was broken and lying on the floor. Remy would not be very pleased I thought.

# The fête-full day.

Finally everyone was up for a late breakfast. Our guests were still tired from travelling over from Yorkshire so we just lazed around all morning. We took a stroll around the campsite. Nathan was pleased he had brought some trunks. The pool was cool and inviting in the hot sun. Remy called out to us and told us that we were invited to the village fête. "Do we need to bring anything?" we asked. "No just yourselves," he replied. "When is it?" we asked. "Now," he said. This was a complete but nice surprise. So we quickly changed into clothes that were more appropriate for a fête. We had no idea what to expect.

We eventually made our way to the village after Sue and Lucy had decided what to wear, It's a girlie thing, that keeps us men waiting patiently, mostly! We followed the smell of barbeques and the sound of music and that led us to one of the back streets opposite the mill. We were made very welcome by a group of ladies who handed us aperitifs. Then the men arrived with a big trolley full of long tables and that was followed by another trolley full of chairs. Remy's van then arrived full of parasols. Other tables were covered with brightly coloured cloths and were laden with home-made pies, cakes, salads and bowls of fruit.

We were told that each family had cooked, baked or brought something for the fête. We pointed out that we hadn't brought anything but we were told we were guests and we should just enjoy ourselves.

With the tables and chairs set up we were shown to our places. What a wonderful afternoon in the hot sun spent eating, drinking and chatting. We were made very welcome. A young couple sitting at our table wanted to try their English, while we tried our French so the interaction was stimulating. We got to know about their lives in the village and their families made us feel at home. I was sitting at the top of the long table looking down the street. I had an irresistible urge to thank everyone. I had worked out in my head the French words, but not necessarily in the right order, but got up anyway and thanked everyone for the hospitality shown to me and my family. I got a round of applause and beaming smiles for my effort, it was a bit of a shock!

Time just flew by as we were enjoying the moment so much. It was just how I had imagined village life to be and I wasn't disappointed. Village school fetes back in Barnsley always seemed to have little cliquey groups who would bitch about each other. Then there were the Ten Bob Millionaires who would look down their nose at me when I spoke in my strong cockney accent. But here in France when I was asked about my roots and I tried to explain cockney the French all had a good laugh at the term.

We were still drinking and mingling late into the afternoon. Just then I saw a small girl next to me get stung. She cried out in pain. The family had no medication. I turned to Sue and asked her if she had packed the antihistamine cream. She told me it was in the tent. After a short run I was back from the campsite with the cream. It soon soothed the pain and the family couldn't thank us enough. My only reaction was that it was no big deal and I was just glad to help.

The crowd of villagers was thinning as they returned to their homes. Sadly it was time to leave but first we helped put the tables away and the parasols back in to Remy's van. As we left we were asked if we were coming to the village party proper that was in a couple of weeks' time. Again we were surprised to be invited but promised we would be there.

The pleasant stroll back to our tents made us realise just how hot the day had been. As we passed each house we could feel the heat that had been absorbed by the white stone walls. We caught the scent of perfume from the rose blossoms. The air was still and the silence only broken when someone closed their shutters with a clanking of the metal locking rods. It seemed even the birds were turning in for the night as there was silence all around and it was so peaceful. I felt very much at ease and stress free as we ambled along. Back in our tents we all slept soundly.

# Neighbours from hell

No surprise that I was first up. The mornings are so lovely and the complete opposite to our mornings back in Yorkshire. I just cannot get over it. I drive Sue to despair as I must mention it every day but when you have worked with extreme noise and traffic for most of your life the peacefulness just slaps you in the face. The tension in my neck and back that has plagued me for many years just eases away.

Eventually everyone was up and we got breakfast underway. Except that for me it was a second sitting with another cup of tea. I had already had a first breakfast while everyone was having more than forty winks. We sat and talked about the fête and how friendly everyone had been to us. Other campers were passing to and fro, collecting water or getting ready to depart after a pleasant weekend. The Sunday afternoon rolled along nicely with barbeque smells streaming in from various directions and a French radio station playing in the distance - with every other record in English.

The tranquility was suddenly thrown into mayhem as the neighbours from hell erupted into drunken shouting and fighting. Remy tried to calm things down and asked them to leave. Then they got aggressive. We offered Remy our help but he was an old hand at this sort of thing although it was a rare happening. He simply called the Gendarmes.
The whole family, mother, daughter, boyfriend, mother's boyfriend and another man were all fighting and trying to stop each other from

fighting. They decided to go swimming to cool off. The mother tried to follow but was so drunk she was on her hands and knees crawling across the grass towards the pool. As she reached a wall she climbed up and hung on for dear life. As she staggered about she was slowly moving sideways inch by inch and leaning into the wall to stop herself from falling over. It was very difficult not to laugh out loud but we didn't want any bother with that lot.

She eventually reached the pool area and worked out how to open the child proof gate. She then walked, fully clothed in a long dress, into the pool up to her neck. If only we had filmed it. It was bizarre!

The Gendarmes arrived, a woman and a man both typically dressed in dark blue combat gear, black polished high ankle boots and utility belts. One very obvious item was the hand guns. It's strange how my eyes were drawn to them. I was half expecting them to be pulled out and in true Hollywood style for them to shout, "Go on punk. Make my day."

The policeman was tall and lean with a close shaved head. His tanned face looked serious and mean as he talked to the marauders from a safe distance. His partner was shorter but was just as assertive in her looks and with jet black hair scraped back to a pony tail. They both stood there with one hand gesticulating while the other hand was poised resting on their hip holsters. It took the pair of them close to fifteen minutes to persuade them to leave in a taxi. They were intent on driving their car but in no uncertain terms they were told that was not going to happen. We happily eavesdropped and could make out a few fast spoken words.

After all the commotion was over small groups of campers gathered to discuss the excitement. That was just as entertaining for us. There was shrugging of shoulders, pointing, raising of eyebrows, pointing with their faces and then the classic French gesture of arms stretched out with palms up and a shrug.

We called to see Remy and he told us that he gave the motley crew a full refund to quash the chance any later reprisals as suggested by the Gendarmes. We later learned that one man from the group was arrested in Caussade. He was known to the gendarmes as a troublemaker. He was a former foreign legion soldier and he had apparently discharged his gun in the town centre. But who knows, the police might just have wanted him off the streets!

# To fly or not to fly?

The next day was the last day for Nathan and Lucy. Their flight was later in the evening so we all had a late breakfast and lunch and took our time relaxing in the hot sun. After lunch they both borrowed our cycles to go exploring. They were armed with plenty of water and the parting words from me saying don't forget keep to the right!

There wasn't much we could do except wait for their return. There was no rush as we had weeks ahead of us to get some more work done on the mill and besides it was after all a holiday with some work thrown in. Sue got some food ready for a departing meal. They returned hot and sweaty a few hours later full of enthusiastic stories of the wildlife they had seen around the country lanes and how everyone was so friendly in the nearby town and hamlets. Nathan's schoolboy French wasn't up to much but I was sure his outward fun loving nature would have overcome any language problems.

Departure time loomed and they were dashing about getting showered and fed. They didn't want to leave but as always in life they were due back to work. Kisses and cuddles for Sue and a bon voyage from Remy and Jocelyne while I started up the truck engine. They jumped in and we were off to Toulouse airport.

We arrived with plenty of time to spare as I drove up the ramp to the departure area. I thought it looked a bit quiet. I gave them both a big kiss and cuddle and told them to be careful driving across the Pennines back to

Yorkshire from Manchester airport and they disappeared through the doors.

Somehow I had a gut feeling so I waited for five minutes on the down ramp. Then my phone rang. "Dad where are you?" "I'm still outside," I replied. "That's good as I've cocked up. The plane went last night!" I just laughed and went in to find them.

A quick turnaround and we were driving back into the campsite. Sue heard the truck arriving at the parking area and walked up to meet me. The look on her face was priceless as we all got out of the truck. After the initial shock we all laughed. Remy certainly found it amusing. Nathan borrowed Sue's laptop and toddled off to the campsite coffee shop to surf the net and find a new flight. We called in to see how he was getting on only to discover the next flight wasn't until the Thursday. So an extended long weekend break it was going to be.

The unexpected stay scuppered my plans to start digging the foundations. It wasn't easy for Lucy explaining to her boss why she wouldn't be at work and could she have a few more days off. Nathan on the other hand is self-employed and any time off work means no pay. I suggested we had a run into Caussade for a look around and to get some extra shopping. It was a bit of a squeeze in the cab of the truck but at least it was less than 10 minutes to Caussade. Once we were in the town Nathan and Lucy went off to explore in the beautiful sunshine while we went shopping. Later in the afternoon they sent us a text and we all met up for our return to Cayriech. They hadn't gone far exploring - it was just to a little bar in the square. The silly grin on Nathan's face told us he had been sampling a few!

After we got back to the campsite Sue prepared another bon repas for everyone. I was glad we had brought everything including the kitchen sink. We had a lovely banquet of tomato and basil pasta, including gluten free for me with a generous helping of parmesan, local fresh mixed salad and I made a stewed plum desert with ice cream. We washed it all down with some local wine and beer. Obviously we all slept well.

We were all late getting up, which is unusual for me. I couldn't understand why that could have been! We just lazed about all morning. After lunch Nathan and Lucy borrowed our cycles again to go off exploring. Sue was relaxing by the tent and I walked up to put some rubbish in the bins next to the car park. Remy, Claude, who comes to the campsite for several months each year, and Jacques, the spy, were standing next to Sue's car. I said bonjour to Jacques who is fluent in several languages, including Russian. They said they were discussing cars and wanted my opinion on the matter. I was taken by surprise but there we were, talking mostly in French, discussing cars. It was a nice feeling being accepted as one of the boys.

Back at the tent Nathan and Lucy had returned from their cycle ride and Sue had prepared yet another tasty meal. We all relaxed for the rest of the evening discussing the day. It was very warm and tranquil. It was a lovely feeling having my son with me enjoying the moment.

Although Nathan looked happy he wasn't settled. We both knew, Sue and I, that Lucy wasn't the one, but you have to let them make their own decisions. Moving to France is going to be a wrench from the family. We could easily move to somewhere in the UK for a change of scenery but Doctors have been telling me for years that I need to move to a warmer climate and it won't do Sue any harm either.

The challenges of our adventure will add a new spark and learning French will keep our minds active. I looked to Sue, I knew she was thinking the same, she squeezed my hand. Time for bed and another restful night.

I get spoilt with the slow pace of the mornings and lunchtimes. They are totally different to our life in Yorkshire where there never seems to be a moment's peace.

Nathan and Lucy said that they had found a nice bar in Septfonds about six kilometres away during their cycle ride the previous day and thought they would visit it before round two of the airport run. They returned later in the afternoon somewhat the worse for wear. Nathan said the bar had had no less than 29 different flavours of beer and lager. Judging by their condition when they returned I thought they must have tried most of them! Walking back from the bar didn't seem to have made much difference to their condition either!

Sue checked the flight details just to make sure before they departed. Another session of goodbyes and they were off back to the cold and rain of Yorkshire. I arrived back at the campsite to a relieved Sue and a bemused French neighbour who was having the airport tale explained to him.

# Don't look now!

Next morning I was up at the crack of dawn. I raced to the mill before anyone could stop me. I was avoiding eye contact with anyone I passed on the way. I wanted to get to work and I know what I am like - a rabbit merchant - if I get talking there's no stopping me.

Once at the mill I was thankful that we only had sun while we had been in France. Any rain would have washed away my painted lines that marked the trenches I was going to dig. I got the new extension gable trench dug first. It was a good four feet deep before I reached ground that resembled something solid enough. I had gone through a layer of small pebbles and a layer of large, smoothed and shaped stone that was obviously part of a much bigger ancient river bed before I finally reached sandy clay. I drove in some pegs to test the ground pressure and it worked out that the width would have to be increased.

By mid-afternoon I had dug out all the trenches. About twenty five meters or so. I climbed the digger over the last one just as Remy arrived. He's come down to do an inspection I thought. "Très bon," he said. "Very deep and big. Why?" I had to explain that that was how I dug foundations. I didn't scrimp. It was normal in the UK on this type of ground.

The heat from the digger cab and the blistering sun was getting to me. I was sure it was getting hotter. Remy went back home while I cleared up. There were huge piles of soil beside each trench that I had excavated, ready to be moved away from the site. A job for another day.

# White wall terror

After making such good progress with the excavations I decided to have a day with Sue. We went for a ride on our bikes until it got too hot. It was also too hot to work. It isn't much fun for Sue when I am doing all the heavy works as she feels a little redundant. I assured her that keeping me fed and watered, as well as tidying up at the mill, was just as important. A tidy site is a safe site.

The campers were thinning out as the French holiday season was almost over. Just a couple of Brits passing through and a Dutch couple who came every year. So it wasn't any surprise when Sue went for a swim and she had the whole pool to herself.

I sat talking to her as she swam up and down. As Remy passed I asked him what the temperature was. He replied 30 degrees. "Phew," I said. He then told me there was a big storm on the way. "When?" I asked. "Now," he replied. It didn't seem possible as there wasn't a cloud in the beautiful clear blue sky. "You had better tie everything down," he warned. Apparently, he had just had a phone call from another site warning him.

It was still hard to believe but we did as he suggested. We went back to the tent and made fast anything and everything. The sweat dripped off my back with all the running around and the sun seemed to be getting stronger. Suddenly a breeze whipped up from the west. We heard what sounded like a herd of animals thundering towards us. It wasn't simply wind but more like air being displaced.

I stood on a chair and looked over the hedge. I couldn't believe my eyes. The only way to describe what I was seeing was to imagine a gigantic white wall as far as the eye could see rushing towards us. Before I could get off the chair the air was whizzing past my face then a few hailstones appeared. We rushed back to the tent and stood in the doorway as all hell broke loose.

We had never seen anything like it. Giant hailstones as big as golf balls fell from the sky exploding as they hit the ground. The noise was deafening and the ground was covered in white in seconds. We saw Remy running in panic to move his vehicle under the canopy, giant hailstones can cause a lot of damage to a car.

A river had started to form on the limestone path with the water getting deeper very quickly. Overflowing, the water headed for the front door of the tent. It totally overwhelmed the path and ran underneath us. We were now standing on a giant waterbed, I am sure if it hadn't been nailed down it would have floated away with us in it.

Remy rushed hurriedly back to us to see if we were ok. We couldn't stop laughing at him. He had his beige knee-length baggy shorts on which were soaking wet and stuck to his legs, a pair of wellies and a small bright red ladies umbrella. It wasn't much use he was soaked to the skin. The force of the hail and rain was going straight through the lot. As the hailstones hit the spare dome tent the hail was projected in various horizontal directions like missiles with tremendous force it was difficult to avoid them.

We then noticed the spare tent was sagging in the middle with the sheer weight of hailstones and was close to collapsing. I rushed inside and pushed up the roof with a broom, running back and forth was hair raising. The hail certainly hurt as it hit me.

We started sweeping as much water back towards the path which was now a raging river. I looked towards the bottom end of the campsite where there was a French resident, Claude who delivered the local free papers. He was living in a caravan there. The water was almost lapping up to his top step. He was looking up towards us from his open caravan door. I could only call out, "Je suis désolé," as we swept even more water downstream towards him.

Remy was trying unsuccessfully to unblock the drains and was still running around with his umbrella with water dripping off the end of his nose. He looked like something out of a Monty Python sketch.

After what seemed like hours the storm calmed as suddenly as it had started. The birds chatted to each other they must have been relieved as we were that the storm had passed. Steam was rising from the soddened ground and the sun beamed down upon us once again, back in business.

# Stake tonight!

The next day, after breakfast it was obvious we had to do something about the mud and grass. It stuck to everything as we walked in and out of the tent and there was still a lot of water about. So we decided to drive in to Caussade to Mr Brico, the local DIY store to get some duck boards. It was just before lunch and the car park was full so we had to park the truck on the street outside. As we walked towards the store I couldn't help but notice a small hatchback car with its boot open. Inside it was loaded with lots of big round sharp pointed fence stakes each about five feet long. I thought nothing more of it except that someone has got some work on.

We found some duck boards, paid at the check-out and went outside. As we left a tall, very slim, young, handsome priest walked towards us. He was dressed in a full length purple tailor-fitted robe. It was gathered around the neck and he looked immaculate. On his shoulder he was carrying a big long, sharp stake. So it was his car that was being loaded. As we passed him face to face I just couldn't stop myself. It just rolled off my tongue in my best French. "Vous avez beaucoup de Vampires en France?" He looked at us, gave a little giggle and then smiled. Sue told me off as we walked back to the truck. I so wanted to go back and get some photos of him but I was told - NO!

We set off back to Cayriech laughing all the way and conjuring up all sorts of images of the young priest with a big stake in one hand and a huge mallet in the other driving it into some poor soul's chest.

Hard at work digging new trenches for foundations

New stone laid & tied to old moulin walls block walls forming the extension prior to building the terrace walls. These are the new internal walls all the external walls will be built in re-claimed stone.

# Shocking trip

We got back to the campsite to find we had new neighbours. They had arrived and set up the tiniest ridge tent opposite us. We gave the middle-aged couple a cheerful bonjour and set about placing the duck boards on the muddy ground. It then dawned on me that my newly dug trenches must be full of water. That was something I didn't need.

I just had to make a visit to the mill later in the afternoon. I was dreading what I might see but was totally surprised to find not a drop of water was visible. It had all drained away and the scorching sun must have dried up the last drops. What a relief.!

After the force of the deluge Remy asked if I was going to the quarry for some gravel and if I was could I get him some so that he could repair his campsite roads. In some places the white gravel topping had just got washed away leaving deep ruts. I had previously been to the quarry, it was just a couple of kilometres away, to see what they had and to check if I could buy from them. Luckily I had a tipper truck as cars were not allowed and also you had to buy in bulk. The savings were enormous against builder merchant prices and their delivery charges. I had worked out the best time to go as otherwise it was grid locked with a convoy of trucks. I introduced myself and got the very helpful weighbridge operator's name.

I bought three tonnes for Remy and he couldn't believe the price I paid. I told Remy to get on the back of the truck and shovel off the limestone into the bare patches while I used my big plate Wacker to compact it down. I then slowly drove to the next patch with Remy holding on and shovelling some more. Blending the road back to pristine condition had him smiling and he was enjoying himself working with me.

While we had a short break I explained to him about the encounters we had in the UK where gypsies called to offer cheap tarmac from a motorway job. Of course, I explained it was just a ploy to relieve you of your cash for sub-standard work and while they were doing the work they would have a scout looking to see what they could pinch. "Ah! he said, "moi aussie. Similaire problème en France." Remy has a deep distrust of gypsies after several problems and on two occasions clients caravans had been stolen.

By the time we were finished it was late afternoon. The sun was still bright and very warm as it set over to the west creating long thin shadows. Remy came to the tent for a well-earned cup of Yorkshire tea and some of my gluten free biscuits. The more we are together the more we seem alike.

The next day I got to the quarry just as the last tipper truck pulled out from the early morning rush. I loaded up with 40mm calcaire (limestone), trundled back to the mill and tipped it in to my trenches to bottom it out with the plate Wacker. I lowered that in with my portable crane as it was too heavy for one person to lift. I had also picked up some foundation reinforcing so I laid that in the trench too. As I was doing that Remy cycled down to see me and he helped me wire it together. It was a bit of over kill due to the mass of concrete I was going to use but belt and braces and all that. I don't leave anything to chance. The concrete was going to be delivered after the weekend so I had plenty of time to clear all the mounds of soil on the land.

I needed some 2 stroke oil from our local hardware shop a few kilometres away at Puylaroque.
It's a very pleasant drive from Cayriech, I hadn't seen any cars, I suppose everyone was just finishing lunch. I arrived at the bottom of the hill to Puylaroque. Turning right at the junction, the road climbs steeply as it sweeps around a very long left hand blind bend. I was juggling the French words around in my head preparing the phrase for what I needed to ask for as the shop owners don't speak English.

I am now two thirds around the bend, suddenly " WHAT THE HELL IS HE? SHI......T " I screamed as I heaved on the steering wheel and threw my 7.5 ton truck across to the right hand side of the road, cringing, as I heard my tools in the back box clashing against the wall of the box. I glanced to my left and saw two big white eyeballs and a very shocked face in a car hurtle past then skidding to a halt.. I looked in my mirrors and thought that was close. I stopped the truck outside of the shop and waved back to the driver whilst mouthing the word sorry! He was still stopped in the road and looking back at me. Luckily my reactions were quicker than his!

Yes! I was on the wrong side of the road. I walked into the shop and completely forgot my rehearsed question, can't understand why!

Whilst driving back to the Moulin I felt a total plonker! I started to go through the scenarios and what ifs. I won't be doing that again in a hurry. Must keep telling myself "Bum in the Gutter" when driving a right hand drive truck in Europe!

I plucked up the courage to tell Sue of my stupidity, she wasn't impressed!

Remy on my truck repairing his campsite drive

Steve compacting the calcaire (limestone) Camping le Clos de la Le're

# War zone!

We spent the next couple of days resting in the hot sun with the odd trip down to the mill. A text from the UK told us that there was plenty of rain in Yorkshire. Nothing new there then. As we walked back through the village we noticed a couple of young boys with a rifle. They were aiming it towards the river but they didn't fire it. I watched them as we walked off to the campsite thinking they were too young and too close to the village.

Back at the tent we settled down for an early lunch. It was very relaxing. We could faintly hear Remy's mum's radio playing. She lived in a bungalow adjacent to the campsite. It was a very soothing quietness then suddenly CRACK! Loud gunfire. We jumped out of our chairs. What the bloody hell were those kids playing at so close. Then CRACK, rat tat tat tat….automatic gunfire. The sound was coming from just over the high hedge so we couldn't see anything. I decided to investigate. Sue said be careful. I hesitantly emerged from our pitch and peered around the hedge at the end of the drive only to discover the village was in full battle. There were soldiers everywhere. I ran back to tell Sue and to get my camera. I walked back towards the village but I jumped out of my skin as I almost tripped over a solider lying in the gully at the side of the road. It was his eyes that gave him away. He blended in so well as the camouflage was doing its job.

As I ventured further in to the village even more troops arrived by truck. They were in full battle kit, firing blanks, shouting orders and taking up strategic positions. I raised my camera to take some photos and a soldier turned, raised his index finger, waved it from side to side and said "Non!" Quick as flash I put the camera away. I wasn't going to upset this lot.

The villagers were going about their normal duties as if nothing was happening. I, on the other hand, was completely enthralled by the commotion. A very tall, large, black sergeant started to give out orders. He pointed with two fingers to his eyes and then to several soldiers. I overheard him say watch my derriere, in French of course, as they moved slowly through the village.

I turned up our dusty track and there were solders hiding behind walls, in bushes and in gullies lying flat on the ground with guns poised. It was extremely hot and they had sweat running down their faces but they didn't move but just lay motionless. Helicopters were flying overhead and also a couple of very low flying jet fighters. The noise was deafening.

Sue walked towards me as she had plucked up the courage to have a wander down. It was a spectacle not to be missed. As we stood in our gateway several platoons walked towards us and as they passed we just had to say bonjour and bon courage. We got nice smiles and nods from them. They turned right at our gate and followed our river. We watched until they were out of sight. They blended in with the distant undergrowth. We presumed they were heading for Caylus, an army training camp several kilometres away. Can Cayriech get any more exciting and special? We will see.

# Our first French soirée

We had befriended the couple in the tiny ridge tent opposite us and it turned out that he was the son of another couple we had spoken to over the last few years. The elderly chap and his younger lady companion, the son and his wife, lived in the mountains and they had come to visit his father for the first time in five years. His father visited the campsite every year from the north. It was nice that we knew them and we always had pleasant conversations, albeit with our basic French. The son told us there was going to be a soirée that evening and he asked if would we like to come. "Yes," we said, "with pleasure."

We arrived just as Remy and Jocelyne turned up. It was a very personal affair and we felt humbled to have been invited. It was also his father's birthday. So it was a double celebration. The aperitifs and wine were flowing. The conversation was certainly testing for us but we were surprised how well we were coping. Even politics and a long discussion about French and English pensions. They were quite surprised how little the UK state pension was. The evening was lovely and still quite warm for that time of the year so we all sat around the table on the veranda of the cabin. The champagne cork popped and we celebrated the birthday and the meeting of father and son.

As the evening progressed, and after a glass or two of bubbly, I decided to tell them a joke, but first I had to translate the various double meanings of the English words. That was a feat in its own right. It was the joke about 8 venison legs I bought in a bar for twenty five euros and did they think it was too dear (2 deer). It went down like a lead balloon. It simply would not translate.

Did they play charades I asked? Blank faces all round. I then had to go through the motions of, sounds like, then film, then book and three words. It then dawned on them. "Charades." I just hadn't sounded the word correctly but they soon put me right. Not wanting to admit defeat and after the next glass of champagne, I stood up. With much gesticulating I told the story of the young priest at Mr Brico. It went down a treat. They laughed their socks off. They really saw the funny side. They even did the actions of driving the stake in and made a silly eek sound. They talked and laughed between themselves about what I had told them. It certainly made up for my poor attempt at the deer joke! The end to a perfect evening spent with very nice people.

The next day we wished our new found friends a bon voyage back to the mountains. They invited us to visit and stay with them whenever we could get down. A nice surprise from a lovely couple.

Strange how this photograph of the siege of Cayriech found It's way onto my computer. This sight must have sent shivers up some spines!

# Solid foundations

Our concrete was due to arrive before mid-day. Remy came down to the mill and said he wanted to help. As we looked over the trenches he said, "Problème." I knew what he meant as he pointed to the deep trench on the far side. With a finger raised in the air he said he had a solution. So we jumped into his van and drove back to the campsite. I followed him into his back garden. He disappeared under a hedge and then started to drag out a huge pipe. The 2 foot x 12 foot long plastic pipe had a cut-out for a chute to fit into. "Très bon," he said. He had used it to pour the concrete for the campsite swimming pool. He flipped the roof panel up on the van and we pushed the heavy pipe in. By this time Sue had seen the commotion and followed us back to the mill on her bike.

We had cleared a path for the big 7.5 cubic metre mixer truck, Sue had cut branches from trees and the pipe was ready and waiting. Remy was poised with his rake and I had mine. We waited for the sound of the truck arriving. It wasn't long thank goodness as it was very hot. We could hear the truck on the other side of the village. I ran down our track to greet him and guide him in reverse back to our mill. After a short discussion with the driver, who seemed very experienced, he fitted his chutes in place. In no time at all we were pouring our first foundation.

The next section was further away so the driver fitted his extra chutes and we positioned the plastic tube on a rock and Remy sat astride it. I guided the other end where the concrete should come out. It was a hilarious sight, Remy's little legs hardly touched the ground, I was sprawled across the other end trying to keep the pipe still and the driver directed the concrete through the pipe. 7.5 cubic metres later and we were done. The driver even helped us to push some excess concrete around the trench to get it level to my markers.

A good job done. I gave the driver a nice drink (tip). He was very surprised. I told him this was normal when we had good drivers doing a good job. He thanked us and was on his way. A fine job done all round. We all returned to the campsite for a very late and deserved lunch.

Later I made a trip to the quarry for 4 tonnes of sand. Then I called at the builders' merchants for a full load of blocks and cement. I wanted to get out of the ground and up to damp proof course. I had brought several rolls of various sizes of DPC from the UK. It was another thing I had to explain to Remy. Damp proof courses only just seemed to be coming into the French Norms (French equivalent of UK Building regulations). Although we had poured a lot of concrete, the trenches were deep so I had to build them up to get above finished ground levels.

Sue was busy mixing mortar while I was laying blocks. Progress was fast. Remy was impressed by Sue as Jocelyne did not do any manual work. Sue, on the other hand, had worked very hard on our previous house in the UK. She stained all the windows three times, inside and out. All twenty two in fact. The biggest job she did was fix the five gable ends with 1,800 slipper bricks in a herring-bone design and in the freezing cold thirty foot up a scaffold. We were determined to move in before Christmas. It took us a year but we got there, albeit with no internal doors, no balustrade for the gallery staircase and the pair of front doors propped up by planks to keep the burglars out. But we had finished the decorating, carpeted throughout, a beautiful fitted kitchen and a raging log burner fire in a big inglenook fireplace. We sat in front of the fire, me, Sue and the two boys on bean bag chairs which we bought from Woolworths. We had sold all our furniture but it was 1st class luxury after spending a year in a static caravan with two kids, two cats and trying to run a busy shop fitting and building company at the same time.

It all came to an explosive head as we neared December. Sue and the boys had flu, the pipes were frozen during the worse winter on record, I was running around like crazy sorting staff and contracts. The pressure got to me one evening in the caravan.

The sink was full, my head was spinning and I picked up a saucepan and smashed every plate, cup and saucer with it. I put the lot in a bin bag and said, "There that's the bloody washing up done." Oops.!

It was all worthwhile as we ended up with a beautiful house.

Building here in France when we move over permanently will be a different experience. There will be no pressure, no deadlines and no clients ringing and asking when I was going to start their jobs. It was something I was looking forward to.

In just a few very hot days we had laid all the foundation blocks for the two foot 600mm thick walls. It gave us a good perspective of the footprint. It would be a livable size. Our ancient mill was very primitive. The remains of a fireplace on the first floor was an indication of how the layout had been and how simple life was for the previous inhabitants who were living above the mill workings.

It would be fascinating to know just how life was at the mill hundreds of years ago. My thoughts were interrupted by a text message. It was from a friend in the UK asking if, by any chance, I was passing his place on my way back England. His place was a few hours north west of us, so a little detour but easy to get to. I text back that it would be no problem.

## Seasonal festivities

The village fête was now upon us. It was a special event - a celebration of the changing of seasons.

A huge pile of wood, branches and brush had been gathered all week by farmers and placed in the paddock next to our land ready for the event. We didn't know quite what to expect.

We strolled down to the village square. It was all dressed with bunting and rows of tables and chairs. The tables were nicely laid with local floral and fauna and place names were set on each table. We were warmly welcomed as we passed our tickets over to a group of ladies at the entrance. We recognised the ladies from the village and we were glad we knew someone there.

The beer and wine tent was busy and the square was filling up fast. The medieval buildings were all lit up with lanterns around the perimeter. It was a magical scene. Remy and Jocelyne arrived. They were on our table as were a Dutch couple we had seen before. They lived just outside the village. The party was now underway. The wine on the table was a nice surprise. It was from a local vineyard and the label had a picture of Cayriech on it.

A band and a duo kept everyone entertained while they all queued for food. It was a long table full of anything and everything edible and it was going down fast. At the far end of the long table was a huge, round, shallow, what can only be described as a gigantic wok about 5 foot in diameter. It was full of a chicken chasseur bubbling away whilst the chef, using two hands, was stirring the dish with an enormous spoon. Beside that was a huge vat of steaming rice. This was going to be a feast. I joined the queue, licking my lips, when I reached the chefs I checked that it was gluten free by showing them my translated coeliac card. I was assured it was. It smelt wonderful. I sat down and was poised ready to plunge my fork into this gastronomic delight, when, whoosh, it was whisked away from under my very nose. The Mayor had apparently had a word with the chef to double check my meal and then had sent someone to retrieve it just in time. The chef had not realised a gluten ingredient had been added later in the cooking. What a bugger! Profound apologies all round and I was sent an alternative meal. Once again we were surprised at the attentive, caring nature towards us in such a short time.

The evening in full swing and we seemed to be getting through quite a lot of bottles of wine. It was then we noticed the Dutch lady on our table swigging away and polishing off yet another bottle of the wine that I had bought from the beer tent.

The organisers came round with some more wine that was part of our ticket. Because I don't drink that much we thought we might take it back to our tent for another day but, before it could be put on the table, the cork was pulled out and a large glass was filled by our guzzling hollow-legged Dutch lady. We looked on in disbelief as her husband then emptied their own bottle. We didn't make a fuss. We just thought next time we would sit next to someone else.

It was a great evening. We called out hello to several people we knew in passing. Our local Farmer Monsieur Rive're came over with his wife and family to greet us. It was a lovely get to know people sort of night.

As midnight approached it was time for the procession. All the children were given lanterns and they held them aloft on poles. Everyone made their way through the little streets following the children. There were lanterns and lights lining the streets on the route to the paddock. A speech was made by the Mayor and the bonfire was lit at midnight. Everyone clapped and cheered. The bonfire was now a blazing inferno shedding light all around. Faces were awash with a warm glow from the fire. All were smiling and chatting. As the flames finally die down all that was left was a huge mound of glowing embers. It was time to go. Another lovely time to savour in the memory bank.

Over the next few days, after tidying up around the mill, we had time to relax. The weather was settled. The ice storm seemed just a distant memory. We had time to chat to neighbours. The young people living at the corner of our lane are very nice. They were of a new age type appearance. Very into nature and they have an allotment next to their house. On most Sundays they have a market stall at St Antonin selling whatever they have grown.

A very proud dad working beside his sons Rory and Nathan

# She's leaving, on a jet plane!

Sue had arranged her return flight back to the UK. The campsite was almost empty. Too quiet we thought. It was also nearly time to for me to go. We loaded the truck with the enormous amount of camping gear which had been necessary for a long comfortable stay. I was leaving the tents to dry after the morning dew. The digger was parked at the camping car park. It was time for Sue to leave.

The usual long goodbyes to our friends was always a touching moment but we climbed in to the truck and headed south for Toulouse airport. I had to come back this way to pick the digger up and then head north. It was a sad journey. Sue would be flying. I, on the other hand, had to drive alone back to Yorkshire.

The journey down to the airport was very pleasant as the weather was very hot. A text was sent back to Yorkshire telling our son to pick Sue up from Manchester. The return text said the weather was awful. She turned to me and said she wanted to stay but she had little choice as her tea room and gift shop needed her.

Our mood was slightly subdued but lifted when we saw the beautiful sunflowers standing tall in the fields next to the autoroute, like hundreds of little beaming smiling faces each trying to see over one another, like crowds of people waiting to catch a glimpse of the yellow jersey of the Tour de France as it passes by.

We arrived at the airport and parked up. I went in to check-in with Sue. My gut instinct was telling me to wait. I was not wrong! Her bags were overloaded. Her cheap return flight was soon to become a very expensive one. In my very best French I asked if we could remove some items and re-weigh, the young lady was very nice and obliging. She even held the queue up while we removed any unnecessary stuff. That was several pairs of shoes, boots, a big bag of costume jewellery and several hand bags.

As each item was pulled out various items of underwear flopped out revealing thongs and bras which Sue quickly scooped up and placed back in her case. The case had to be weighed several times. I don't know how she squeezed it all in such a small travel case in the first place. The check-in girl found it very amusing. A woman behind us, speaking in Spanish, was getting agitated and tried to move forward but she was sternly sent back and told she had to wait. Our friendly girl carried on helping us and finally Sue was checked in with big smiles and thanks. So we were heading for the boarding gate. I hadn't been looking forward to this moment of saying goodbye to Sue but it had to be done. I watched her make her way towards the gate and out of sight.

It was a very odd feeling driving and arriving at the eerily quiet campsite on my own. Remy was waiting for me at the gate, he must have heard my truck approaching.

I gave him a wave as I parked next to our pitch and started to dismantle the tent and load up the last remaining bits of building kit ready for leaving. It was close to five in the evening. "Did I want to stay the night?" he asked. "No its fine," I replied, "it would be too strange on my own. I would rather be on the move. Remy said, "You must eat." He wasn't wrong there as I had missed lunch and burned a lot of energy off. He sat me down at a table and set about cooking Toulouse sausage and chips for me. It was obvious he didn't want me to leave. We get on so well. Finishing off the hearty meal with a coffee it was time to go. I hitched up the digger and with sad goodbyes to Remy and Jocelyne I roared out of the gates with my roof beacons flashing and a loud blast from my air horns.

Once again leaving Cayriech was difficult. The people, the river, the wildlife and the pace of life make me dread the thought of returning back to the fast pace and noise of Britain. I slowly drove through the village and over the bridge for my usual last look at the river. A few sad thoughts and I was soon on the autoroute heading north. I planned on stopping at the jardin services near Cahors for the night before heading north west towards Perigueux.

As I entered the services area the truck park was filling up quickly. I managed to get a space but it was a Friday night and some trucks wouldn't be leaving until Monday. The air was still and very warm. The sun was only just setting so I had time to wander around the park area which was set in a little sunken valley with a pond and plenty of wildlife. Looking across to the church spire it reminded me that some years ago, when we first came to France, it seemed to us that nothing really changes there except time. Looking forward to a new day, I finally drifted off to sleep in the cab of the truck.

# New day new journey

The bright sunlight rising above the valley woke me from a deep sleep. I quickly got ready and grabbed some cereal before going into the services to see what was cooking. Just for a change I had a fried breakfast and a cup of passable tea before departing to Rouffignac in the Dordogne.

The journey across country took me through some lovely terrain and sweeping valleys with the buildings changing slightly. The colour of the stone used for the buildings was a light brown stone whereas in our region it was white stone. The route took me through a very busy Gourdon. As I passed by the main town that was rising up high on my right. It looked very impressive in the soft brown stone architecture. I had to keep my wits about me, traffic was coming from all directions. There were lots of people about. It must have been market day. I didn't need to stop but it was certainly a place for a future exploration.

Making good headway I passed through Sarlat. It never ceases to amaze me how beautiful France is, every turn of the road reveals another breathtaking view or wonderful building that seems to be preserved from the past. There can't be much more to impress me.

I spoke too soon! As I hit the historical Les Eyzies de Tayac - wow! Prepare to be impressed when you visit. The vastness of the cliff and rock faces complete with ancient windows and doors carved in to the rock face and clinging pathways leading up and seemingly defying gravity. It got more breathtaking as I drove below an enormous protruding mountain of rock that was just hanging there like a huge shelf. I held my breath and shuddered, thinking that if that broke away now it would be curtains! Of course it didn't. It was obviously a big tourist attraction with endless coaches lining up. C'était très occupé. Yet another place we will have to explore one day but out of season.

Lottie She's a big softie really.  Photograph by Neville Stott

# Camping take two!

I finally got close to my destination, Rouffignac, a town raised to the ground in 1944 by the Germans in retaliation for actions by the French resistance. Just the church and a house was left standing. It had been completely rebuilt by the Germans as part of war crimes negotiations after the war. It was nice and twee in grey granite. Very prim and proper. It wasn't what I expected, sort of old but sort of modern. I wasn't far from the hamlet but I had to ring the UK for specific directions from my friend. I soon found it after driving past the sign that was only visible from one side. It happens a lot in France. I managed to turn around under the watchful gaze of an old farmer as I reversed into his drive. He didn't seem to mind. He just gave me a wave as if to say well done lad good driving.

I turned up the very narrow lane with the trees either side swishing past my windows. The lane opened out to green fields that revealed a small cluster of little houses, a Hamlet. They were built from excavated volcanic rock boulders that were rough and resembled clusters of honeycomb. The boulders were carefully placed with only gravity holding them together. They were in deep reds and shades of dark browns. They also had well weathered exposed oak timbers in places so they all looked ancient. I parked up and went in search of my friend's neighbours. They had the drawings for the work that was required.

Their house was next door to Rod's, my friend's barn which was going to be converted into a new home. The neighbours, John and Yvonne, had a long house and several stone pig sheds that they had converted and restored over the five years that they had lived there. The buildings were set around a rectangular courtyard which made them very cosy and private. The design was very French. I rang the brass pub type last orders bell hanging by the wooden gate. I was given a warm welcome as they were expecting me. After introductions they produced the drawings for the new road.

John explained the drawings to me. It was pretty straight forward. The road was to be about 100 metres long and about 2.8/9 metres wide with a turning point. I rang Rod from my mobile. He was in the UK. I told him excavation was no problem but we would need about 60 tonnes of 30/40 to 0 mm calcaire (limestone). A deal was struck. I could get him calcaire at a good price and all done at mates' rates. I would start straight away.

I rang Sue who was by now back in Yorkshire recovering from her flight. I told her I wouldn't be home for another week or so. She was a little disappointed.

I unloaded the small six man tent and rigged it up. I just got out the very basic camping gear that I needed. John let me plug in to their electric though we had to use three extension leads and luckily I had my motor home 20 foot lead, otherwise I would have been in darkness for a week, or having to endure the constant noise of my generator.

The plot with the barn on it was perched on one side of a very big hill top, quite exposed. It was an ancient volcano and the soil was a heavy deep red.

By the time I had got set up darkness had fallen. I was also very tired and very hot as the temperature hadn't dropped below 27° and with not a bit of breeze all day. I slumped onto my camp bed, I text Sue good night and I was off with the fairies.

# The long road ahead

The intense light woke me at six thirty. I was wondering where I was at first then taking some time to come around. I had better get cracking I thought as I had a lot of work in front of me. Then I remembered it was Sunday. People don't like noise on Sundays, not before 10 am at least, so I checked the digger over and worked out a plan then marked out a starting point. I started digging and made good progress through the high banking by the lane. I had the truck parked next to me so I could I load it up ready for tipping in piles at the corner of the field.

At the end of a very hot day I sought out John. I needed information to see where the nearest quarry was. It turned out LeBrug was the only one nearby. As luck would have it John knew a short cut through the forest logging roads. It almost cut the journey in half. He accompanied me to LeBrug the next day as he had an idea where it was but wasn't sure. As it turned out, we couldn't miss it. In the distance was a huge scar of white where the hillside had been scraped away. We got there just as they were closing for a two hour lunch but at least we knew where it was.

We arranged to call for a load of calcaire the next morning. As part of thanking my helpful neighbours John needed a load for the finishing touch for their swimming pool which they had installed themselves. We tried to pay cash, but "Non," tried credit card, again "Non." Cheque or account only, so cheque it was. I was relieved I had my French cheque book with me.

Now that I knew the lay of the land I went back to order three twenty tonnes loads. Not a problem or so I thought. Wrong! All the trucks were twenty two tonnes running out of the yard and all were contract drivers. If I hadn't remembered some building terms involving delivery etc., I would have been in trouble as no-one spoke English. Twenty two tonnes loads were not a problem but when? Could be next week or the week after as the contract drivers I spoke to were fully booked. No one could be specific. There was only one solution which was to collect myself. Whilst talking to the drivers there was the usual shrugging of shoulders and raised eyebrows and that was me! I was picking up the French way of talking - so some progress of integration.

Le Bugue, south of Rouffignac, was a busy town and to reach the quarry I had to use the only road through it, then over a train line and over a bridge. During my fourteen trips that hadn't been in the equation and I had to make a few detours after the council decided to close the road and resurface it. One day I had to turn around and go back after sitting in traffic for an hour. I could only manage two trips before lunch and two after but at least I was getting the job done. The new road back at the barn was dug and I was reversing up it and dropping four ton loads off at intervals.

The council was just finishing off the new road when I got stuck in the traffic again. A big articulated tipper passed me, then reversed and wiggled in to a very tight spot. The driver climbed out of the huge Renault Magnum tractor unit. You know the truck, it's like a block of flats on wheels. I sat there open-mouthed as the driver was a young pretty petite girl with long dark hair tied back in a pony tail and a baseball cap. My only thoughts were – go, girl, go! She certainly deserved the job. Top marks for French woman's equal rights.

I spotted a wild boar on the way back from the quarry one day. It was running next to a fence. I told John about it. Oh! It's a wild boar farm. My little bubble burst.

I was getting low on hard cash so I tried to get some at the bank. I walked in with a cheque only to be told "Non." I can only draw cash in the Tarn et Garonne. That was something I didn't know. I didn't have a French bank card.

I took a trip into Rouffignac in the evening to use my UK bank debit card at the cash machine. It was one of those senior moments. I keyed in the wrong pin number three times and it locked out my card.

I had very little cash left and I needed to fill up with diesel. It must have been one of those days when things go from bad to worse. The petrol station at the supermarket rejected my credit card and my debit card despite there being plenty of cash in both. I offered to pay by French cheque and it was accepted thank goodness.

The credit card worked fine everywhere else on the way home - so bizarre!

The days were long and very hot, mostly around 30°. Finishing off just before dark gave me time to get a hot shower under the stars. My solar outdoor shower came in very handy. It must have been a sight for any peeping toms with me running about naked. Especially the day I forgot to hang it in the sun and had to get a cold shower. I moved like lightning. Working in the blistering sunshine, I didn't just have a tan I had red skin as the deep red soil was staining my skin. Perhaps I should have worn a feather in my hair and done a red Indian rain dance. It might have started a new Dordogneshire craze!

A French couple out on a walk, they were from Le Mans, stopped to speak to me. During the conversation about what I was doing and where I was from and also explaining that I was building a house further south in Cayriech they were resentful as to why so many Brits didn't integrate in the area but stick together doing things the English way. I explained that it was the same problem that we had in the UK with the Asian race. It does cause problems but nothing can be done as the problem is too big and deep set. Another little insight into French thinking. It was nice to have a pleasant chat as it was a little lonely working on my own all day. In the evenings I was so exhausted I just flopped on my bed and zonked out, except for one night when foxes and dogs barking somewhere over the hillside kept me awake.

Waking in the middle of the night for the loo was very eerie. I was glad I had a portable loo so I didn't have to go far in the pitch black darkness.

John and Yvonne invited me round for meal. I had a nice bottle of wine to take and it was a lovely evening, so nice of them. They had kept out of the way so I could get on with the work and were not the interfering type but very friendly and helpful. The job was going smoothly until one day when I tried to go through the normal forest route to Le Bugue. It was completely blocked by logging lorries with huge Hiab cranes. I had to go the long way round on the sightseeing route and along the south of the river La Vezere. I was getting very familiar with the roads and the surrounding area.

I took some time out from building the road at the little hamlet and popped into Rouffignac for market day to replace my dwindling supplies. It was a typical French fresh produce market with lots of different stalls and a few market garden stalls

Listening to the cheerful conversations as I mingled taking in the sights and smells
In the sunshine and open air. Watching the characters getting into discussions about parsley with the stall holder or tasting cubes of cheese, then telling the stall holder how much they wanted indicating with their thumb and forefinger. it's such a civilized way to shop.
I bought a couple of fresh chicken thighs that I planned to grill back at the tent.
I had a peaceful evening listening to the wildlife whilst tucking into the chicken with salad so fresh I could have just picked it!

The weather changed suddenly, strong winds blew through the night. The tent heaved too and fro between the gusts, I heard the satellite dish blow over, it clanked around for a while or maybe I fell asleep. The next morning was eerily quiet, no bird songs, no wind, it was very strange. I went outside and looked around. I was surprised to see fog rolling in, slowly it surrounded me and the hill, it reminded me of the horror film The Fog. It certainly was an odd atmosphere.

After a late trip to the quarry the weather changed again, the sun slowly appeared as a hazy ball at first then burst through, burning up the remaining mist.

I was now nearing the end of the job. All the immediate neighbours around were Brits except for one house along the road which was having work done by French artisans. The builders ignored me just driving past every day but would have a good look at what I was doing. I had a wander during my lunch break to the house they were working on and it seemed that progress was very slow but the workmanship was excellent.

Just a couple more runs to the quarry were needed. I had built up a good rapport with the loading driver and he knew exactly what I needed.
I would drive in and on to the weighbridge, drive off and get loaded, then back on to the weighbridge and finally off back to the hamlet. I had left an open cheque at the office as it kept things simple.

One day I arrived and a new driver was in the loading shovel. I called up to tell him what I wanted and how much, shouting over the noise of the machinery. A thumbs up and "d'accord" from the driver. I watched in my mirrors as he loaded. Thinking that was it, I was about to pull away when suddenly he dumped another tonne of calcaire in my tipper. The back dropped. I thought something was going to burst. I got out and called over to him. I just got the usual raised eyebrows and a shrug.

Now I was overloaded, so I would have to off-load the excess weight somehow at the quarry. It was a quiet afternoon so I decided to chance my luck and drove very carefully back whilst keeping a watchful eye out for the gendarmes. Panic over and off loaded. The next trip my regular driver was back - thank goodness.

Keeping in contact with Sue in the evenings kept my sanity. I tended to talk to myself a lot and in French. Simple words but French all the same. I was very pleased when Sue told me the weather back home was picking up. I don't think I could have faced the cold and rain after being spoilt here in France.

The work was tough in the hot sun. After working over there I could understand the French two hour lunch break. Walking up and down the road with my heavy plate Wacker compacting the calcaire in layers the break was completely necessary. There wasn't much shade on the hill top so I was constantly drinking water.

# Leaving for Blighty

It was now time to leave. I got an early start packing up but it still took several hours. John and Yvonne said goodbye as they were off shopping while I continued to load up the digger. When they returned they were surprised to see me still strapping everything down. More goodbyes and I was off.

As I started to move off the land the artisans working at the house across the road drove slowly past. They gave me a thumbs up followed by big smiles and a wave. I don't know whether they appreciated the work I had achieved on my own or were glad I was leaving. Another Brit working on their patch. Who knows?

The long journey back up to northern France on a new route took me through undiscovered places. I had often seen the sign for St Yrieix la Perch, I think I was expecting a magical place but the road just went around the town. It was Friday and the roads were very busy, I didn't make time to stop and discover or explore because I was on a mission to get back to the UK, although in my heart Cayriech was becoming my spiritual home and Barnsley was just where we were living.

As darkness descended, the roads got longer and lonelier. The last hour towards Calais seemed never ending, my eyes were heavy and playing tricks on me.

Finally, in the distance an amber plume of light hung over the autoroute surrounded by the blackest of nights, I gave a sigh of relief as the torturous journey was almost over. I turned off the autoroute and made my way to the truck park and fuel station where I planned to spend what was left of the early morning.

I had a shock. It was closed down. The new petrol station and parking area were fenced off and boarded up. A lot must have happened in the eight weeks since I was last there on the way down.

I was very low on fuel so I drove to another all-night unmanned petrol station close by in a large industrial area. It was deserted and very dark, hardly any street lights. I pulled in between the pumps, it was very tight for my truck and trailer. After filling up and just pulling away one of my trailer's tyres clipped the metal pump surround base. I had a sickening feeling and with a cry of "I don't believe it" plus quite a few expletives, I ripped the new tyre I had fitted at the farm back in the UK.

It was 3am, I was exhausted and tired, but I just had to get it sorted. I had a spare wheel for the trailer but it was almost flat. Being a true boy scout I had a portable compressor and was able to pump it up. Jacking up the heavy trailer with the digger on was easy as I had a 5 tonne jack. I was cursing myself for being a complete plonker but this is what happens when you are tired and pushing yourself.

Finally I was on the ferry and exhausted at 5am. I was relieved to be able to get some hot food from the Transport cafeteria and have a rest, I sat mumbling to myself under my breath. I must have nodded off, I awoke with a start when the docking announcement over the tannoy interrupted my dream! I was soon on UK soil.

I stopped at the nearest lay-by to try and get some sleep before heading north. Except the early sun rose fast, my truck swayed from side to side in the lay-by as juggernauts leaving Dover passed by, I wasn't going to get any sleep here, besides, the bright sunlight gave me a second burst of energy.

# Surprised faces!

Several hours later I arrived in Barnsley, the weather was warm and sunny. Nothing seemed to have changed while I was away, familiar faces going about their business, as usual.

I was back but it wasn't Cayriech!

Thankfully I was able to park in the side street next to Sue's tea room and gift shop. I walked through the door to the tea room. Sue and Rhona were very surprised to see me as they hadn't expected me back until Monday. Regular customers seated at the tables having lunch started quizzing me. They were asking how much work I had done at the mill and so on. I kept everyone entertained over lunch delighted to hear my stories.

We were together again in our little flat with our two Siamese cats Jazz and Blues. As the evening fell we missed the tranquility of Cayriech. The noise of speeding cars was constant and the sound of strangled wailing tones echoed around, it was karaoke night at the nearby pub.

Our adventures, trials and tribulations, highs and lows over the last few years since we embarked on our French house hunting trip, was only just a beginning.

We still have a long way to go before we move in to our new mill house but life is built on dreams and aspirations.

It's what keeps us going, new horizons and new challenges. I have a saying, "If they can get men on the moon then everything and anything is possible." It's just a state of mind.

## The End????

No! The beginning of another chapter in our lifetime.

# Acknowledgements

Thanks to all my family, especially Susan my wife whom I have driven to despair with my constant questions and remarks, how do you spell, or, that's a stupid looking word and who only got to read the book in the final stages and gave it her invaluable proof reading. My two sons Nathan and Rory, who have had to endure my outbursts and frustrations of never having time to finish this book.

To our wonderful friends. Peter and Eileen who have lived the stories in this book with us, but they don't know it yet, because I haven't told them the full extent of their unwitting participation!

Phillip (Pip) Prior who took me under his virtual wing so to speak and edited my dyslexic scribbling.

Special thanks to (in no particular order)

Remy and Jocelyne, Alan & Viv, Neville & Louise who without their friendship life in France would be like any other town, friends like these make a place worth living in.

There are so many virtual online acquaintances far too many to list, I look upon them as friends, who have given me support and encouragement over the years to keep writing and eventually writing this book, I salute you all.

To the village residents and Maire of Cayriech who made us feel welcome.

Kim Prior, Artist, for the wonderful watercolours, we will treasure them for ever.
The beautiful watercolour on the back cover was painted by Kim using my CAD designs of our Moulin and sketches.
Kim has captured exactly the design, and colours we were looking for in our new house
See more of Kim's work at www.segur-prior.eu

The artist drawing of our Moulin by J Bergere and more information
www.les-petites-toulousaines.com
Larrroque Immobilier Caussade France......www.immolarroque.fr

**Proof & Beta reading by**

Julie Haigh (Hawkeye) & Anne Wine O'clock Durrant.

Thank you both for giving up your valuable time!

The list below represents a wealth of information that is available online.

Forums with like minded people giving their time for free to help with anything and everything wherever possible.

Plus a couple of useful links

www.motorhomefacts.com
www.thefranceforum.net
www.motorhomefun.co.uk
www.frenchentree.com  formally Totalfrance.com
www.hobosinfrance.com
www.frenchexpats.com
www.motorhometoday.co.uk
www.practicalmotorhome.com
www.motorhomehq.co.uk
www.ukcampsite.co.uk
www.wildcamping.co.uk
www.the-anglo-french-forum.co.uk
www.lost-in-france.com
www.completefrance.com

www.rhumetal.de   Autohaus Rhumetal
www.camping-leclosdelalere.com

# EPILOGUE

Would we have done things differently?

Yes and No!

We should have done it years ago is an easy thing to say in hindsight but we can all say that, you get into a rut, and then something or someone, as in our case, just makes you push that button.

Above all our family came first before even considering leaving for France entirely.

House and location.

I wanted to live on a hill overlooking the sea, we ended up in a valley next to a river, but the place and location is fantastic, you have to be flexible and open minded when looking in a new country or you could waste time and money looking for the rest of your life, while life passes you by.

Worries about the language barrier.

None whatsoever, Sue stands by with the dictionary and phrase book, I do a lot of arm waving and inspector Clouseau impressions and draw pictures in the air. The French we have met everywhere have been so helpful and patient, they seem to sense we are trying, or just amused....but seriously, Sue has worked hard at learning French, but it is very important to learn some very basic words relating to property purchase, technical terms and suchlike and recognise them written down.

The building work to be done.

There is no escaping the fact that there's a lot of work to do but it's no more than what we have done in the past except we are older luckily the pace is slower in France, then there is the sun and the wine to compensate!

## Why Captain's French Adventures?

The nickname Captain was given to me many years ago by a workmate, who contracted to me on building sites.

   Almost always on Friday afternoons I would slope off invariably when we had a difficult job on, I would be heading for Hull and the North Sea to board a Yacht and setting sail for my sailing course, Trevor  would shout out, "There he goes Captain Pugwash, don't worry, I will carry on digging this hole" laughing as I went..

 So my nickname didn't come from a famous captain like Drake or Cook, but the TV cartoon character Captain Pugwash. I did end up being a qualified Skipper though! So my nickname has stayed with me and I use it on the Internet forums.

Author Steven G King

Made in the USA
Charleston, SC
28 January 2015